Being Human

in the Now

Conversations with the
soul of my sister Ajra

Ana
Pogačnik

Translated from the German
Menschsein im Jetzt –
Gespräch mit der Seele meiner Schwester Ajra

Translation by
Sibylle Kort

published by
InterActions
Stroud UK
contact@interactions360.org

English edition
Copyright © InterActions 2022

ISBN 978-0-9528364-6-9

Layout and Editing: InterActions
Printed in the UK

Contents

Introduction 7

How this book came to be written 7

A few more words to the contents 8

Words from Ajra for the beginning 11

The conversation with Ajra 13

On the drawings 113

About the authors 115

Acknowledgements 117

Other books 118

Ajra, you were and are a bright light,
which accompanies me always.
It is a great gift,
that I can be so close to you.

Ajra's presence

Introduction

How this book came to be written

My sister Ajra was not only as a mother, sister and woman a great human being, she was also a spiritual teacher, author and exceptional, irreplaceable healer. She dedicated her life to healing on various levels. From our perspective it seemed that a severe illness took her far too soon from life. It was comforting for our whole family to know that as such a highly developed soul she would be able to support us all 'from the other side' in these crucial times.

Since her transition in the year 2011 I have sensed her presence, sometimes more intensely than at other times. I nurtured an on-going connection to her but did not know how I could deepen this contact.

In late autumn of 2020 my father, Marko Pogačnik, found many unpublished messages, notes and sketches of Ajra. These were messages she had received from her spiritual master in preparation for her seminars, in response to posed questions and explanations to themes, which either she or Marko had wished to understand. At the beginning of Ajra's active spiritual path, she worked for some years intensively with Marko. Marko had the idea to make a collection of Ajra's texts and to publish them.

This thought did not leave me alone, until I understood why I felt so uncomfortable with it. I asked myself: How would I feel if I was in her place and suddenly someone came up with the idea to publish my notes, preparations for my seminars and all unpublished messages, from between thirty and twelve years ago, in a book? So I said to my family: 'I would rather burn all of it myself now so that nobody could one day get the idea to do just this.'

Hence one evening I asked Ajra to give me a clear sign how we could solve this differently. I awoke in the night and knew that I can connect with her as a soul and in this way give her the opportunity to actually comment on what it means to be human in the NOW. I was relieved because I understood that she has much to say and that she wishes to help us humans in this difficult situation.

The writing was very intense, and I used my family-free evenings to prepare this book. Up to now I had never written a script with such speed – the bulk of it I received in less than a month.

Already whilst writing I sensed the necessity to give these messages to people as fast as possible, and herewith I follow this impulse.

A few more words to the content

This English edition is being published a year after the original German edition, and due to this time difference incorporates an additional question which I put to Ajra. This is noted in the text.

In a few years' time we will most likely be laughing about the intense situation we currently find ourselves in. At present we are still with severe restrictions in place in many countries – life has been sort of put on hold and our freedom further restricted day by day. Globally unbelievable things have been happening. The world is finding itself shortly before a revolution. One thing is clear: it cannot continue like this. But how will it continue nevertheless, and what are the big changes that are needed?

As humanity we are standing most certainly before something New, but it is still very difficult to imagine this, to form a picture of it. What can we personally contribute, how can we support the process?

Life has generally become so superficial, and the world is being increasingly governed by lies.

It is clear that we human beings hold a very important and central role in the life of this earth, but what hinders us to break out of this monotonous life? How does the path of an inner revolution look like?

Where are we heading as humanity? Do we still know this at all? We have such huge potential and could receive much more support, if only we would open ourselves to this – the world of the presently not incarnated souls, being an important part of humanity, is waiting to give their contribution for the mastering of the current tasks. So much strength is lying dormant; if only we would open ourselves towards yonder world!

During this volatile world situation I got the opportunity to pose questions to a soul who dwells in the all-beingness. I did not consider the questions beforehand; they came quite spontaneously, out of the intimate connection I keep with Ajra, so to speak. One theme announced itself after the other, and our communing developed from there.

I am able to sense Ajra's presence directly and to communicate with her inwardly. I do not hear her voice, I do not see words, but can write down her message as thoughts that flow rapidly towards me. Whilst I am writing – when I am directly in the flow – it does feel to me as if it were my own knowledge. But I know that they are not my thoughts, because also for me some things are new and surprising.

As with any such messages, the statements are nowhere written down as fixed messages. The meaning of the content arises within the energetic flow which streams from Ajra to me, which I then translate through my presence into words. Hence I am conscious of the fact that I am a filter for this translation. Someone else would clothe the stream into different words. Therefore I dare to call myself the author, although Ajra herself is the true author.

Please give yourself enough time to read, so that the power which lies in and behind the words, will truly reach you. Through these words speaks and works the spiritual eternity, which flows towards us through Ajra's presence and her written messages.

It is not about just understanding the information but about being moved, touched deep within our soul. The words can become like a channel of light through which we can expand ourselves and so can reach and grow far beyond ourselves. With Ajra's help we as souls can travel through this channel of light. As a soul we do know how it works and how we can grow through this.

As help we can inwardly do a somersault before reading - we can imagine it in such a way that we perform this somersault from our heart into the head. In this way the heart space can stretch and expand into the brain space and the impulse to read with the heart carries over to our mind.

Herewith I have fulfilled my part of the task and am happy that the gate is now opened.

Feel free in what manner you will get yourself involved in this journey of discovery.

I wish you much joy, many deep experiences and much inner width whilst reading and even more so in life.

In profoundest gratitude and joy.

Ana

Original German edition, January 2021.
For the English edition, 26 January 2022

Words from Ajra for the beginning

Life on earth exists in two parallel worlds: one part is visible, is incarnated, materialised, hence it is known and accepted. The other part is for most people not within 'reach' and lying beyond their existing reality.

At present much more weight and importance is given to the visible; however, the invisible carries much more weight for the soul and impacts so much stronger on both our personal and collective stories.

Why is this part concealed? Why denied, ignored? Why can they not talk about it in schools, and why do we not learn about it as children, why are those who are engaging with it not being taken seriously and not to be believed? Why? Why is the most important part kept in obscurity?

As incarnated souls we can tentatively gain some view of what lies 'behind the scenes', can sense or possibly make out much of what might be happening in the invisible dimensions, but we cannot really experience it. We can only do this once we ourselves exist in the non-physical sphere of life. The viewpoint then becomes totally different, and no one can imagine how different it is.

It is not that long since I myself experienced the transition from one side to the other. Therefore the earthly life is as yet not so far removed from me, not to know how strong an influence it does have on you as incarnated human beings.

I am here to make the invisible side of life visible – life then appears absolutely different, so much looks completely different in this light.

I am here to answer unanswered questions. I am here to make the knowledge of the other non-incarnated life visible and with this also to make the visible side a little bit more 'invisible'.

In so many respects life is portrayed in a totally false picture, because the larger context of life is still being ignored. That which we as 'normal' people experience in daily life is just a small crumb of what true life consists of. It is really an immense pity that the big mystery of life is mostly veiled over for us. Today the spotlight is too strongly focused on the material and hence the essential part of our existence remains un-known to us, un-reachable, and sadly we do not know how to 'use' it.

This could be the starting point for our conversation – I still have the possibility to indicate out of my own experience how you could direct the spotlight where it is more beneficial.

You, Ana, pose the questions and I will answer them. I am ready, that is what I am here for. Let's begin.

23rd November 2020,
with amendment for the English edition, November 2021

The CONVERSATION with Ajra

Let us start in the present situation. As humanity we are standing before a huge change. I have this image: we are standing at the abyss and have the opportunity, to jump courageously into something as yet unknown, unimaginable, and thus to save ourselves – or we fall into the abyss. Both are real possibilities. What is certain is: we are at the end of our previous possibilities - we cannot continue on this level. What is happening right now?

Yes, the abyss truly exists, but only if we look solely at human life on earth. This changes if we look at the whole flow of life on earth and in the spiritual world. On the spiritual level there is a waterfall, but no dangerous abyss. This means our existence is neither extinguished, nor is life interrupted.

It is true that as humanity we are facing a huge test. Will we be able to jump, even whilst not knowing where to? Are we ready, and how many people are needed so that we can manage this jump collectively?

Most importantly, as you say, we have to be conscious and clear that our old ways are at an end – they cannot lead forwards! As humanity we cannot continue in the same way! There is no bridge across, nor a detour that could get us to the other side.

Therefore there is no outer solution in this situation; the only path begins deep inside of us – we have to take the reins into our own hands and out of our full potential perform the quantum leap.
We do not need to be acrobats but – to stay with this metaphor – everyone can and should be ready to make this inner jump.

As humanity we have never witnessed anything like this before – so we have not learned how to do it, but we are all capable of it. Hence in crucial moments we as human beings are able to widen our consciousness to such an extent that, whilst remaining human, we develop superhuman capabilities.

No less is required here. In reality we have access to the inner core of life and by the same token to the purest life force. We have the capacity not only to use this force but to activate it within us – it cannot be more direct.

What is outwardly happening right now on earth is scary, not as much due to the events themselves as to how people react to them. Instead of understanding that it cannot go on like this and it only being a question of time until this old construct collapses, we still believe that there is a road to salvation via the old and well-trodden paths. That road does not exist. And looking at it from 'outside' I can see that the Old does not have the power – it just pretends to still have that strength. On the spiritual level the decision has already long been made– only the New can win.

Now it is up to you incarnated human beings to decide how and where the path is – how long you wish to hold on to the Old. You decide how long you wish to artificially keep alive something that is so to speak dead.

Life cannot exist any longer in the frame of the Old and certainly will not be able to flourish – hence it is clear that the Old has to make way. Unfortunately, the transition this time will not be so smooth or self-evident, but that does not mean, however, that the Old can keep its power.

In the background a battle is being fought between forces for and against life – a battle fought since over 2000 years, that now reaches its climax and therewith its conclusion. In the invisible spheres it has been decided already and it is clear that those forces undermining development and growth of life cannot and will not win.

The one who sees and knows these facts can observe the outer happenings in relative calm, as it is clear that only life can win.

 How comforting to hear this and yet I ask myself: what happens in this scenario with humanity? Do we come along; will we manage? Are we far enough, are we ready? Do we really still have that direct access to the core of life within us, as you say, or have we forgotten or even lost this possibility?

Yes, we will manage. You perceive only the incarnated part of humanity, but we are so many more. We have been all waiting for this moment for such a long time, how could we miss it now?

That is impossible. Here is an image: you are crossing a desert and are close to dying of thirst, and when you then reach the water, instead of taking the last step, no matter how much effort it asks of you to reach the water, you give up.

As humanity we cannot do this! The spiritual world will not allow this to happen.

You are fighting with yourself and against each other, instead of finally realising that this is no longer the point.

It is time to gather all our strength collectively to bring these counter forces to a halt: they are attempting to stay in power with all means in their possession – though this was not their original plan. We can manage this only if we become aware that they actually do not possess the power to win – with this consciousness we will conquer them!

These forces have enormous power, are literally mighty, but still they cannot win, as at the end they will sabotage and weaken themselves – they will fight against themselves. There is too much that is untrue, twisted, artificial and disingenuous living in them to be able to voluntarily transform their own nature.

They will have to confess and therewith lose face. They are not prepared to recognise how they disturb the development and destroy life; they cannot step voluntarily into their own transformation but will need to be accompanied into deep levels of transformation.

For you as incarnated humans the most challenging step on this path of liberation is to comprehend these forces – to identify them behind their masks! They are so clever; they have kept spreading themselves more and more and have incarnated together with humans deeply into the material world. That is why they are so strongly interwoven with humanity that often we cannot see and recognise them anymore – they have become so much part of our world that we do not experience them anymore as dangerous, as hostile to life and ourselves.

This is the biggest danger. The counter forces have crawled so deeply under our skin that we are almost not able to recognise them anymore. They work through humans without being directly part of them. They can use them as tools and are in this way deeply woven into humanity.

This is the reason why humanity cannot easily wake up but needs to be downright shaken out of a deep sleep.

All humans who have acted against life, no matter in what way, in this or a previous life, carry within themselves through their stored memories something like a docking point where these counter forces can dock. In this way they can use us humans as a gateway to enter into our human world – in simple words, they can work through us. We could say that each of us potentially holds such a spot in our memories which can be exploited.

How many of us are conscious enough on our personal journey to have already transformed such spots? How many are conscious of how quickly and without our noticing we can become an extended arm to the counter forces? Many people think this is impossible, but when such a docking point is active within us, we cannot easily notice how we get 'occupied' by counter forces. It happens faster than we can think. It is precisely because they are so deeply rooted in our human sphere that they do not appear to be hostile: they are within our sphere and so inside of us.

This will be one of the biggest tests for humanity. Only those who recognise the danger and consciously free themselves will be awake enough to follow the path into the New.

At the final 'releasing' these powers will drag with them into the abyss all people who are too deeply and closely entwined with them. This does not mean the end for these people, these souls, however they will have to undergo a very deep and painful waking up process and fundamental transformation before they can re-orientate themselves inwardly anew. To wake up in this way takes considerably longer, is more painful and laborious, but many will not be able to escape this sorrowful process.

And this takes us to the part of your question whether as humans we still have direct access to the core of life. All human beings have once had the key, but unfortunately in many cases it got lost in one of many lives. Of course, this does not mean that it cannot be found again!

This direct access to the purest life will be decisive in the near future. Only if we are in touch with purest life can we gather our own strength and so recognise the counter forces.

These are two decisive steps that we are involved in as humanity right now: to get consciously into our own power and to recognise the counter forces.

This sounds serious. We are led into our deep and painful points, there as wounds, and we will not be able to act or "do as if'. This means we are confronted with all the unresolved issues within us. What is important to know both personally and as humanity? What can we do to speed up the inner liberation, the personal process? What do we need to know?

Most important is the consciousness that we humans are beings of light – due to our nature we are dedicated to the light. If we follow our origin we will always orientate ourselves towards the light. The question, though, is whether we are inwardly still sufficiently free to do this; but within our true spiritual self our compass always points towards the light.

This is an exceptionally important characteristic of human beings. Thanks to this alignment we are guided, accompanied and protected.

If we are conscious of this, we will ALWAYS find the way into the light, without getting lost. 'We are beings of light, we are beings of light, we are beings of light.' – this should be like a mantra for us in the coming time. It will carry, strengthen and help us to stay in the flow.

And it is true, at the moment there is no time for masks, games and un-truths – ALL will be swept to the surface and will confront you. There is no other way. As humanity we are facing a huge leap and for this leap we have too much baggage – we are simply too heavy to be able to jump.

We need to relieve ourselves, we should and can liberate ourselves from it. It helps so much to take this as a gift rather than a burden.

It is so good when, finally, all becomes visible, although it is not always pretty. But then it is out and cannot be hidden or swept under the carpet any longer.

This is a time of truth! Anything that is not the whole truth needs to be viewed and transformed. And as has already been said: all that does not get transformed voluntarily, will be in one or the other way 'forced' to do so. As you can see it does not make any sense to be stubborn, as this transformation will not pass us by – we humans will not be able to escape it.

How can we perceive, keep and be true to the light in these dark times? How does it look from the other side, can you help us to see more clearly?

As non-incarnated souls we do feel the light because it is our true substance. For you incarnated souls the light is integrated into matter. This does not mean at all that it is weaker; on the contrary, it has to be even stronger in order to shine through matter, to penetrate and radiate through it.

The light is materialised in humans. We are materialised light! Every morning we should remind ourselves of this before we start the day. We are not the heavy matter, which weakens the light, but materialised light.

If we feel and experience ourselves within our physical body – it is maybe more difficult to imagine this, but that which continues on when we leave the body after death is the light; and that which anchors as a seed in matter at conception and develops throughout the embryonic phases, incarnates and in the end materialises is also light. What could show more clearly that we are light?

Particularly when around us life is darkening and the air is getting heavier it becomes ever more important to not only feel the light, but to let it also radiate!

"Do not seek the light outside, because you will not find it until you recognise yourself as light." This almost sounds like a well-worn spiritual phrase, but isn't it so true and so essential at the moment?

Absolutely. This is and will in the coming times be the distinguishing feature. Everybody, yes everybody, will have to decide on which 'side' to stand. A clear confession of our convictions will be demanded. This lame, half-hearted stance, half sun half the darkest shadow, grey instead of radiant light, will be over.

The more consciously we incarnate the light, the easier it will be to stay faithful to it.

To the question, what do we stand for, a conscious answer, a decision will be demanded of us. But the question will not arise within us so clearly as a question. Possibly people will not even realise that they are dealing with this question. They will be able to demonstrate their decision by deeds and behaviour rather than with beautiful words. This is why it is so essential that we consciously nurture the light, live it and radiate it even more consciously.

Can you please say some more to this important decision? Everything seems to stand and fall with it and we need to be well prepared. Are we talking about the decision for life?

It is more than only a decision for life. We have to resolve to say yes to a new life, for life on a new level. Of course, life could continue on the old level, but it would be a life without an access to the new vibration. It is about readiness for the quantum leap. For this we need an inner decision and a decisive inner and outer effort. This is the decision for exponential growth, for fundamental change, for a profound transformation, which is not achieved only by this decision, but only starts to unroll.

All presently incarnated souls will have to confront this question.
The question is not about whether one is capable or not, but that we decide for it, no matter the consequences.

In our present situation in the world this will not be an easy decision, as the attitude will not fit into the mainstream frame. That means very possibly that because of this decision we will be looked at strangely, ridiculed or even excluded.
Exactly that is why it is so decisive that our alignment towards the light and the New is unshakeable.

It is now not enough to think: I wish to move into the New rather than to remain and stick with the old – that is far too weak. That is absolutely not enough! You will too easily get wobbly knees and much too readily get caught by outer and inner fears; you will too soon be ready to follow the main stream.

This decision we face as humanity is a decision for something Big – and for this our readiness likewise must be BIG.

Is it possible we still don't get that we are dealing with a dimension of change that is totally unknown to us? I realise by myself that I do not have a real imagination of how big it is. I believe we imagine a change within our known frame of reference, as a cosmetic adjustment.
Of course, we hear that the world will be completely different, but being right now incarnated here on earth it is really difficult to let go of our known imagery and to launch ourselves freely and openly into something we have no notion of yet.
What could help us? How can we become freer? How can we burst our constraints to view the world anew beyond our known parameters?

It is not entirely true that as humanity we do not know such major changes. We have made and experienced similar leaps. I consciously say 'similar' as none has so far been this big.

In the time when as human beings we were physically not yet incarnated on earth we went through big changes and crossed many portals of different dimensions as a civilisation. But that is very far and distant for all of us, and our present materialistic phase of life is so strongly engaging that our memory does not stretch that far back. But as cell-memory we still have this stored within us – which means on one level of our being we carry it within our cells.

The less baggage we carry from either former lives or this incarnated phase of human life, the easier it will be for our soul to refer back to this knowledge in our cells and the more flexibly and faster we will be able to adjust to what is happening.

It is not a coincidence that everything is 'boiling to the surface' right now – as already mentioned, we are being confronted without mercy with old stories, painful grievances, unredeemed situations and unresolved relationships. We are in the midst of a general cleansing.
If we can see this change in conjunction with the larger change of life, we can understand, accept and follow it better. We have to become freer and lighter!

Maybe it helps if you dismissed the urge to see this new world already now. That could remove the pressure.

You should keep your focus on the materialised, deeply incarnated life and earthly consciousness, as you need this right now to be able to take the necessary steps as humanity.

Once the process has advanced so far that we will be ready for the inner opening and speeding up of becoming conscious, it will happen step by step, so that those who have so decided will have the possibility to be part of it. As long as this does not happen you will not be able to see the New. It is still invisible for you because it is still beyond your reach.

It is so important for you to be conscious of how huge, decisive, overwhelming, indescribable and over-dimensional this change or, better expressed, this fundamental leap will be. Then you will take this current process of transformation more seriously.

The feeling of humanity united

As the currently not incarnated souls, we are here, too, as helpers in this transition. We do have a sight into beyond, although the coming upheavals are in many ways still un-known and inconceivable also to us. We as souls also stand before something entirely new, even though we can see further – and even though we are less limited.

We are passing through this portal together and we can support you already now.

Please stop seeing us merely as deceased, stop grieving for us, missing us as physical presence and lamenting that we are no longer physically incarnated next to you. You do not need to feel sorry for us! If you do so you exclude us, you deprive us of our strength, you take away our opportunity to be active, you shut the door in our face! Please!

We are One – we are one humanity, we are one unity. We are still one. No, we do not stand on two different sides, neither on two different levels, nor do we move in parallel worlds. We are one unity. We are still together and united we walk this path.

It is true, you are incarnated and we are not, but this does not need to separate us; paradoxically it gives us the chance to unite even stronger.

There is nothing that can separate us – not even space and time, which in your material world seems to be named as the main cause for separation of incarnated and non-incarnated souls.

This is a burning call to you as incarnated human beings. We need you and equally you need us. It is not a coincidence who is or is not incarnated right now. We need each other, because only together can we walk through this dimensional portal. Just as little as we can pass through it alone, so you can also not pass through it without us. Only united, together, will we be able to take this huge step.

 It is a big theme, I think; there is so much involved in this separation. Through the course of time so much fear of death has been imparted on us humans, so much burden projected onto this transition, so many promises given, so much grief added, so many taboos created, so many doors closed, so many

tears shed, that it is not just a massive separation, but more a wall of silence, of grieving and departing that has been created. It is actually absurd and yet this has become part of the 'normal' in everyday life on earth. This wall grows thicker and more massive every day – how come?

Why did we lose this unity with you as humanity? And my most important question of course, what can we do – each one in their personal life and also collectively?

I wish to be totally honest and tell you what I see and experience when I observe everything from my wider perspective of life. Unfortunately this is part of the plan of the counter forces, to weaken us as humanity! Just imagine how we would stand as humanity in the world if we would be united? – Yes, exactly, we would be invincible.

For the other side, working against the progress, this is too dangerous. To divide and separate us was the simplest way to half our strength.

It is easy to look back and track how human beings always had contact with their ancestors, with the non-incarnated souls, and lived together with them, so to speak. The beginning of this separation was approximately two thousand years ago; what a 'coincidence' that this was just at the same time as the 'war' between those forces which work for life and those which oppose the development of life. This is very obviously a trap into which we as humanity have stumbled.

There is still something crucial that needs to be added here: if we keep this separation of the visible and invisible souls intact, we as incarnated human beings also lose more and more the connection to our own invisible part. This separation has grave consequences of which we humans are not conscious.

Not only are we being robbed of strength but also of hope, and our trust in life is weakened; the sense of being-one is taken away and much more.

This is a huge wrench in our development. We are more and more losing our self-independence.

When death ceased to be seen as a threshold from one life to another but instead as an end, our image of what life is changed fundamentally. The nebulous, unclear, insecure, unknown, invisible which comes after life was represented more and more palely until it was slowly extinguished. In its place appeared instead a black hole into which we all disappear after death.

I consciously show it simpler and 'catchier', because in its essence it was really meant, planned and wanted like this.

If we believe that we disappear with death, that death is the end, that of course colours our entire life in its very foundations. It interferes seriously with our image of life, with our idea of what and how life is. It takes away our trust that we are carried by life, but it also takes away the depth of life – as we then seemingly only have this short span of just one life.

What many people like or even take as a relief is the fact that any responsibility for our actions is in a way taken from us. If we do not believe in life after life, there would be no unpleasant confrontations, clarifications nor consequences for ourselves or our environment after life or in another life. Everything disappears in a black hole.

But how do I live my life carrying within my consciousness the thought that at the end everything I ever experienced will disappear and dissolve into thin air? Life loses much of its vitality, a part of the beauty of life is taken away from us. What sense does it make to strive to do the good, if at the end it all disappears apart from what is in the memories of others?

This of course gets even worse with the idea of 'an evil' death, which has been forced on us and is even being used to threaten us with. The truth could not be twisted more effectively: as an individual we are kept small with lies and a wrong image of this incredible life portal and therewith the transition. And as humanity we are separated by what should be a connecting portal. Can it get more absurd?

Death is such an important part of life, which we need for our development like the air we breathe. How can it be that such an idea of death is still being used in order to keep millions of people in check – who believe they will be damned and abandoned by God if they do not adhere to certain rules in life?

Who has the right to say something like this, and more importantly: would anyone say such if one would be working for the good of humanity? No one! Behind stands clearly an abuse of the force of life.

We as humanity have been separated through this. We have lost our common human sphere – we have literally been robbed of it.

I assume we will get back to this theme, seeing that it is so central for us as humanity. The connection to death and to the non-incarnated human beings forms us much more than we can imagine. It colours our entire presence and being.

But so far to give a short answer to why it is so.

Maybe it is most important to talk about your question what we can do to achieve a change.

It is crucial to understand how we arrived at this separation at all. Only then can we grasp what it means for humanity and what we can actually do. Again we are dealing here with the theme of waking up.

As humanity we need to bury as quickly as possible these distorted images of death and their meaning in a deep black hole – I say this consciously so sarcastically, because it is so painful to be separated like this. It hurts me when I attempt to get in contact with currently incarnated souls who were even close to me in life – and when I, as a non-incarnated soul, am not seen, sensed, understood or heard and often simply being ignored. Even though I know that this is often not due to those people, who really do not hear me, but due to the collective image that humanity has of the beyond – this does not change the painful fact that we do not have each other anymore. Even more painful because I can see that it is only a trap we have fallen into completely! This is an evil game, and we are the victims in this game.

It is high time that we wake up and notice how we are being manipulated through these wrong images of death and the price we ALL are paying for this. Only we can change this - you and I are doing it right now. Nobody will show up one day and say: sorry, this was really not very nice of us; you are allowed to unite again. Let us evermore, increasingly, reach hands to shine through, break through and dissolve this barrier.

It is essential to find again a new realistic and friendly image for this transition, an image that helps us to forge a healthy relationship with the life after life. As you can see, I consciously do not say life after death.

We can do much, but we also need to be prepared that much will change in life through this. If we are not ready for this, it is safer to stay in the cage. Our foundation of life has been consciously deformed to guide or rather manipulate us. Once we correct this, we will of course also have to adjust the constructs of life built on the former. These will all be good changes, but it is particularly these that can often not be the easiest to bear.

I believe it is worth delving even deeper here because, as you say, we do not notice how we are guided and governed by false images. This is so central for our human nature. But maybe such false and distorted images of death can influence us so strongly only because we have forgotten our own death experience in the process of our new incarnation. Therefore we have no inherent images, feelings or 'proof' that it is different, hence we can so easily be led astray.
Could you help us and give us a new image, what happens to a person when one dies as a human being and steps as soul without a body into the life after life? What kind of process is this and what exactly happens with us then? There is no doubt plenty of literature, but I would like to hear from you first-hand how it feels. Could you bring this experience closer to us?

This will be a bit longer of an answer.

When I myself was within the process, I wished I had known more about it, because I was also influenced by the collective wall and due to this blocked on many levels. The fact that in this life on earth all is coming to an end is of course in that moment alarming, and

Into the power of the All-being

everything within me contracted. So it was a lengthy process for me to come out of the inner solidification. It paralysed me inwardly and in many respects I was not myself anymore – I could not be myself, because I was no longer free and was also strongly affected by the collective iron curtain. In such a process this is of course very unhelpful.

Once I had battled through this – you accompanied this battle of mine very closely and strongly and through this helped me a lot – I was in a certain moment suddenly able to let go. It is really a similar feeling to when you hold a balloon on a string and at a certain moment you let it go, let it fly freely into the sky.

It is important that we make this decision by ourselves because this strongly influences the whole process of detachment. Sadly today this is not anymore self-evident due to medicine attempting to 'save' the human being up to the last breath – with this we take away the option of making this vital decision. Through this the natural process as well as the further course of the journey are severely disturbed.

I myself expected at the moment of letting go a concentration of energy and with it a narrowing, but I experienced the total opposite: it is an inner liberation, because the whole width and breadth of the soul is unfolding again.

What we call the death process, we can truly compare with the metamorphosis of the pupae into a butterfly. Everything comes together, and this on all levels – all has to be translated, prepared, summarised. Everything that we encountered in life and that we have stored, that has touched us as a soul and is important for our further development, is gathered up; out of this a cocoon forms, within which we can experience the inner transition. This process is slightly different when someone is going through an unexpected and sudden transition and death.

This moment of emerging from the cocoon is for the butterfly, for the soul, something imm ense, as the weight falls off and the soul is born again into eternity.

This however does not mean that the soul returns immediately into the

All-one. The process of the detachment from matter needs time, just as the journey of the physical body at birth and the incarnation process need time.

The first moment of detaching is an extraordinarily strong and striking experience and an enormous release for every soul, but then a very intense phase of detachment begins.
In a few words, one could say the soul works through everything that has made her into an individual personality throughout her lifetime.

It is a process in which the soul finds herself again fully within herself, in the deepest core. This is more difficult for those souls that in life did not show their true colours – who did not follow themselves, their own true nature. It means in this case a long and arduous searching and rediscovering, until one finally arrives again within.

It is like a mill through which the soul goes and all information, 'adventures', memories, images, experiences gathered throughout life of a soul are ground more and more finely. The soul needs this time to carry and translate everything from one dimension into another.

This is easier the more consciously the human being has lived in life, and the more challenging the more unconsciously life and the transition have been experienced and lived. If we stay with the metaphor of the mill, in the latter possibility there would be many impurities up to large stones among the kernels and seeds. Hence begins the purifying and processing connected with it, a clarification and sorting before the real grinding can happen.

It is not well known that the soul, although no longer living with the physical body, still needs its body for a certain period – namely partly as nourishment, orientation, also as anchoring and to still transfer the stored and gathered impulses. It is literally like an umbilical cord that facilitates the on-going connection to the material world and the physical body. This connection dissolves naturally once the link becomes unnecessary. Very often the body is taken away from the soul too soon. This is not healthy because an abrupt loss of the physical body also means a hastened removal from matter – this can lead to a 'precipitate birth'.

How the whole process unfolds depends again strongly on the entire life as well as the experiences in former lives. Likewise it depends on how much the soul can lean on her human circle from life, how processes of clarification continue to happen and how the whole surrounding from her life on earth is able to hold a space for the soul to be able to release fully.

As a metaphor we could picture a tree deeply rooted in the earth, having spread its presence all the way into the tiniest roots. In the same way a soul extends herself everywhere with her presence – and so her process does not only relate to herself but also to the process of detaching from all fellow human beings or more precisely fellow souls.
This is a very complex event. Maybe I am going too far in my explanation, but it is not as simple as often presented: a human being dies, gathers and dematerialises – and that is it.
It is a path, which according to our human way of measuring time takes a few years. The soul withdraws her presence more and more from the roots, from the material, working through her experiences and then literally dissolves.

This process, of course, is not only simple and beautiful, because as a soul you get to see everything experienced on earth from a different perspective. On the one hand this is beautiful, on the other hand painful as you witness other interrelationships, because you recognise what as human being you were not able to see, understand and feel.
The truth is no longer wrapped in cotton wool, is not transfigured with the help of various excuses or simple explanations – as for example, that you did not really know what happens or the like – but you are faced with the naked truth, with all feelings, emotions, images and facts that belong to it.

You see yourself in a mirror, which knows nothing but the truth.

This process is a huge process of maturation for the soul as only through this review can she grasp all life's interrelationships in their depth.

Once the soul, thanks to this process, has ripened like a fruit, she is ready to return to the width and breadth of the All-One. This is a necessary preparation because the soul would lose herself in the All-One if she had not before this found her way back to her true self and her innate purity.

Once she has arrived in the Width, she is completely beyond the material existence and therewith loses the direct access to matter.
The soul remains gathered and centred in a kind of own focus, but she is not anymore confined – she is now beyond all space and time constrictions, which we humans are subjected to.

Back to your question: this transition is a celebration, a metamorphosis, a birth, an enormous experience for the soul – the crowning of a life. It is much more difficult when we do not know this because then we are not prepared and are in many regards lost. Most of all, though, we miss the celebration of life. This is the harvest for our soul, because only then do we truly recognise and experience the fruits in their entirety. Hence the celebration of the process of dying should be something akin to a harvest festival. This celebration does not relate in any way to grief or loss, much more to abundance, gratitude and inner joy.

I am not trying to say that the farewell does not hurt and that the loss of dear people is not allowed to be accompanied by sadness. Of course also this is a part of the process of detachment and needs to find its place and space as well.

Important though is that we do not allow ourselves to be overwhelmed by grief, so that we lose our connection to the soul of the departed and give ourselves over to the force of separation. The danger that this happens is potentially big, particularly due to the collective programming, which we still follow in this connection.

And it is just this that is the crucial point, and which is so important, because it is up to us as human beings to change it. Otherwise we impede ourselves on this path of development. To remind you: only together can we master this step lying ahead of us – humanity as a unity!

 This is really fascinating. By now we know a lot about experiences of the soul during birth, but the process of dying

is still shrouded by a grey veil. In the depth, we know and understand so little, and I believe it is precisely this that blocks and slows us down more than we are conscious of. Because it is nebulous und unclear for us, we associate so many fears with it, which brings us back to the manipulation, which can happen at just this delicate point.

If I understand correctly, are the so called 'ones left behind' an important support for the soul in this process? How does the soul experience this help? Can you speak from your own experience?

The soul remains for a while in an in-between space – the physical body has been abandoned but the sphere of the soul-eternity has not been entered yet. I have already explained why, to be able to manage this process of working through everything, the soul depends on her access to concrete people, places and experiences and such access she receives mainly through people she knew. Of course, it is also from other beings and companions. These are important ports for mooring and pillars for the soul, because here she can maintain direct contact to life.

The soul has to harvest her fruits, otherwise they will be lost for her. Particularly in the early phases of detaching from matter, the people she knew in her life just left play a key role. They are like gateways through which the soul can still enter the space of concrete life in order to fulfil her own process that is needed for her growth.

If these people disappear behind a veil of grief and fear of loss however, they are not really fully present in their own lives and cannot be a support for the soul. They are too much lost themselves to be able to offer the space to this soul, which she so sorely needs. For a soul going through such a profound process, this is a decisive loss, as she can no longer get the access.

If people would be conscious, that precisely such a situation opens the opportunity to generate a new closeness, new relationship, a new togetherness with the deceased person's soul, they would in many situations act radically differently.

From the viewpoint of the departed soul, the endless grieving is a great burden and a rather egotistic 'fuss', because it is for the soul difficult to understand that just at the moment when she would need a helping hand, she meets deaf ears and lost eyes.

The dividing wall between visible and invisible worlds is scarcely comprehensible from the soul's perspective – especially because the separation appears so abruptly.

Of course, the soul will find alternative possibilities to continue her path regardless. But at first it is difficult to accept if you suddenly are not understood any longer and are being viewed as if through a thick pane of glass – to such a degree that the soul realises she does not exist for the fellow people anymore. For the soul the world as such continues to exist, but the physical sphere acquires a totally different shape and hence a changed appearance, and yet all is still present as before. This is why it is exceptionally challenging to simply accept this separating wall.

I personally was accompanied, heard and supported, but when I imagine this differently, I would have felt quite abandoned. The people we have known believe they are being abandoned by the departing soul, but in reality it is they who abandon the soul, because they cease to nurture the contact and exchange with the soul. In this way, they unconsciously position themselves behind a collective dividing wall, and render themselves invisible and unreachable. How fatal: although both sides long for closeness with one another, both feel abandoned and cannot find each other in this confusion!

It is time to break through this wall of silence and separation and transform it into a sphere of unity.

Though we all know that this circling between life and 'life after life' is something totally natural, that our course of life is comparable to the four seasons, that this transformation from visible to invisible dimensions is important – yet particularly when young people die we often hear: 'she was in the midst of life'; 'he was wrenched from life'; 'she was taken from us by this evil

For immersing ourselves deeper into the stream of incarnation

sickness'; or 'he still had so much to give but had to go'. How does this happen? Is the soul being called home at a certain time? Does she receive a higher call, meaning she has to go now? Is she being surprised, or do we as soul decide when the moment has come?

Before we descend to incarnate on earth as a soul we have planned a certain orientation for the impending life. With this we know what as a soul we wish to learn in this life. In tune with it we are being given a role in life, which then gives us an opportunity to become wider as a soul and to grow. What up to now was completely misunderstood: even the manner in which the soul masters the transition is part of the training, which we have anticipated as our task.

The soul is never being wrenched from life or will never be punished with a serious illness or catapulted out of life. Never. The soul decides on the course of her life only and alone by herself.

But it happens often, that a soul herself decides or chooses an illness to serve as an emergency break. If a person deviates completely from the intended path and potential learning opportunities, the soul might use the illness as a means of correcting or if she does not see any further chance for readjusting even use it as an emergency exit.

I do not want to generalise though. A soul can definitely choose a serious illness for a learning process or a 'reset' in the midst of life – which could then be seen as a new beginning or almost like a 'new incarnation'. An illness can sometimes also develop, so that the soul may again find herself or get to know herself deeper. There are so many varying facets, hence there is no sense in prematurely claiming, judging or, worse, projecting anything.

I cannot stress enough, that a soul, or rather to say a human being, will never be punished with an illness, nor any suffering ever be inflicted from without!

But there exists also something like a soul-calling. The soul is not being called home directly by a higher authority, but she might be called because she is needed on the invisible side of life for specific reasons. Just at the current time this does happen again and again because certain souls are better integrated and needed during this important leap as non-incarnated souls. Even this does not mean, however, that the soul is being steered from without; it should rather be seen as an inner call.

Precisely this alternating between visible and invisible phases, active and 'passive', incarnated and non-incarnated realms of life, offers the human being a great potential for learning and growth. We would never have chances to experience so many and mostly such diverse roles, aspects, sides and experiences if we were constantly incarnated to the same degree in the material world.

Out of this rhythm of changes the opportunity arises to enter into most diverse situations of life. This gives us as souls and human beings a breadth, which we otherwise would not be able to reach. Everyone can experience the most diverse aspects of life and hence enrich oneself as well as the collective consciousness. This makes us so special and unique.

Growth, maturation processes and the expanding of our being are potentised through this. Both the intense phases of direct experiences in life and the subsequent phases of processing these – enabling us to integrate the experiences into the stillness of the universe – are equally important for the soul. The one without the other could no way lead to such an enormous gain in strength.

As human beings we have a double nature and we need to be able to live both, else we would fall out of balance. We need the earth because we are the earth. Equally the earth needs our presence on the earth, as we co-create her and are an important part of her consciousness.

At the same time we are also cosmos and need the cosmic phases, during which the soul lives her cosmic 'quota' whilst not being held and formed by the gravity of earth. We are able to unite the earth and the cosmos by living through these two alternating intensities.

We could imagine ourselves as a ball of light that moves between the earth and the cosmos, continuously connecting the two spheres. At one instance we are nearer the earth and practise her knowledge, with the next throw we are nearer to the cosmos being enriched by the knowledge of the stars.

This on the one hand sculpts us as soul and concurrently the earth and the cosmos are being connected and interwoven through us.
If we stay with the image of the ball of light, we can envisage all incarnated and momentarily non-incarnated souls as such leaping balls. This constant alternating, the uninterrupted exchange, the eternal movement is like the planets, which move in the universe, weaving the life. This is a wonderful, moving and touching image.
We are incredible beings who bring so much light into life.

How can it possibly be, that exactly such incredible light beings are capable at the same time of so much darkness? Looking at the current situation on the earth... we do have the choice as humanity with regards to what we wish to support, bring into life and incarnate. How can it be that precisely now so much aggression, brutality, impudence becomes apparent? How does this look from a wider perspective? Being right in the middle of this, one cannot do other than shake one's head and wonder how this is possible.

Yes, this is indeed a big question. Why do we need this dark side? Do we really need it? For our process of learning we do need it. The confrontation with it is an invaluable help for more deeply penetrating the material world.

However I do need to emphasise that it is not as it is often shown to us: namely that, because the earth allegedly carries darkness within it, we as human beings on earth bring to expression this darkness. The truth is the total opposite: the earth is a being of light that embodies love. This is why we can practise our fighting nature on this planet – because at some point, namely, we will be 'conquered' by the love of the earth.

There are two aspects that I would like to mention in this context: one is the personal component. To find the strength of the middle, we practise within both extremes, right and left – so also in light and darkness. It is essential for our growth to be guided through varying experiences. We serve the light or the darkness and consequently work for or against life. We ALL as human beings have lived through phases of both aspects, otherwise we would not be able to continuously develop ourselves in the direction of light. We need this maturation through our personal experiences of both sides.

The other component is the fight, which we have witnessed over the last two thousand years. We humans are of course involved in it, we live our own personal stories, we grow and become more and more conscious and more and more filled with light. We talk here about a larger framework where we do not just view human history but the events in the great wholeness. At the moment you are experiencing the intensification of this battle on earth.

After these two thousand years the light and life and all interconnected forces are about to ascend to a noticeably more intense level. Through this, unimaginable possibilities are opening up for the growth of life – this is the quantum leap, for which we are preparing right now. This puts naturally a spanner in the works for the powers of darkness, as they are about to lose the possibility of direct influence. Up to now they have always found ways of being active, right into the level of matter – they always found a sufficient number of people whom they could get with their claws and tentacles, could work through them and could therewith actively influence their decisions.
If Life now will be lifted onto a higher frequency, they cannot directly co-create any longer. That is why they are fighting right now so mercilessly and desperately for their survival.

We humans are standing right in the centre of this battle, are being played against one another, are being exploited, abused and scorned. We should observe very closely what is happening so that we will know how to act in this situation, that we don't end up being deeply wounded during the very last stretch of this battle.

Knowing this, we cannot however simply excuse the deeds of those people working currently in the hands of these forces – because they do join in actively, they are as souls responsible for their actions; but it helps to remind ourselves again and again of the larger context, in which these forces seek their paths through people.

At the same time we should not forget that the counter forces are indispensable for our development. In an amplified manner, they mirror for us the darkness, heaviness and unredeemed elements still residing within us. If we take them seriously in the right way they will even be our guides. Through them we can understand better in which direction we do not want to go and hence know the alignment we wish to choose as soul.

They are indeed relentless, impertinent, they are brutal and know no boundaries – and yet they are meaningful and precious for us human beings. Right now we are learning unspeakably much from them as humanity.

Yet how can we protect ourselves against them, so that we do not fall into their hands, so that we do not become their tools or get hurt through them? What are our possibilites to recognise them and their energy?

When I observe you humans through my 'eyes', you are an intensely radiating light sphere, surrounded by a slightly dimmer shining layer of light, and this again surrounded by a weaker one and so on. This means the soul is enveloped by several layers of light and thus protected.

The more actively the true strength of the soul is being lived, the stronger the light of the soul radiates; the more conscious a person lives his own presence, the stronger is the soul's light and the less vulnerable he is, because the protective layers are also stronger. Due to this the dark forces cannot interfere so easily with this radiating light.

At the same time I have to say that such a radiating soul is particularly attractive to the dark forces – they feel drawn towards her, because this human being radiates so much light and is therefore dangerous for them.

Hence in their 'game' it is important to weaken such souls. Of course they would love it even better to win over such people. Hence they do not leave anything untried to con them and pull them over to their side.

So how can you protect yourself?
The first step surely is to radiate and expand your own light. Maybe even more important is the inner cleansing. The less impure – dark – spots we have within us, the less opportunity we give the dark forces to take hold of us. Such places within you I perceive as dark shadows that dampen your light.

In this context we need to be conscious of the following: as said before, we have all already lived in some lives on the dark side and that is where these shadows originate. These are memories, unredeemed fractions, non-redeemed relationships, which are not yet sufficiently penetrated by light. These shadows are like knots in your light-body, which are not permeated and therefore are disturbing your stream of life and flow of energy. We do know what happens in the physical body when we have such knots; something very similar we can perceive on the level of light.

When we wish to live our light, when we wish to serve the light with our whole being, such purifying becomes imperative. Otherwise it may simply be too dangerous to open ourselves up to the light – we would sooner or later involuntarily become a victim of the dark side. The dark forces are continuously on the lookout for such shadows and spot them instantly – the same attracts the same. The smallest impurity may suffice for them to at least attempt utilising this as an entrance.

The other important thing, though, is to protect our light in such a manner that we enhance it and radiate it outwards, yet simultaneously radiate it inwards as well and thus intensify it. In this way we anchor it more deeply within ourselves. We not only expand the light outwards but also double its strength in our inner core. For those around us it generates an extraordinary light-effect in which the light refracts within itself in a special way, so that it appears less visible. It dampens itself, so that to outer appearances it looks less bright than it really is. In these times while the dark forces still have so much power, this is a ploy which you should not underestimate as it can very well protect you.

It is not about hiding or diminishing our light; on the contrary, we only want to protect it when and where necessary.

What would help us to be conscious and awake in these times? Many do not want to know what is currently happening, but rather only want to look ahead. Many still believe everything the media tell us, many continue to sleep...What is important? How can we safeguard ourselves, also through expanding our consciousness? How does all this look like from your perspective? Are you able to see who among us is awake?

Ohhh, and how I can see this and even more so sense it. I am not limited by space, which means as a soul I am present in the All-Being. Although you people exclude us souls from humanity, we are of course nevertheless part of it and sense so extraordinarily strongly what is happening right now.

We do not view your individual deeds and movements, we do not look upon you continuously to see what you are doing, because we indeed are too occupied ourselves. But we sense the collective mood very clearly – we experience it within our being, we experience it as a reality that concerns us and our existence very severely.

It is incredibly difficult to reach people that are enveloped in unconscious sleep. One can shake them, but even this they would not notice. To sleep-walk through life means not to be entirely incarnated on earth; the consequence is, that such people are only half present and hence only half consciously perceive and experience the world. This is not meant as a reprimand, but it is an unalterable fact.

Due to the many unresolved karmic narratives, which stretch through several incarnations and stack up energetically within our bodies, it is the current common tendency that incarnating into matter and hence into life, into the body, is not happening completely.

When we observe closely, we experience that a complete incarnating cannot occur at all. Those souls that have too often lived their lives unconsciously have currently a very challenging time, because too much has accumulated within them and access is becoming more and more difficult.

Yet right now the time has come to work through those old stories, to clarify them and so to clear up our foundations. If this does not happen, it will be harder and harder to withstand the intensity of our current time. The way we do this is not so important; important is only that a thoroughgoing purification and transformation takes place.

Many people render their senses insensitive because they cannot bear this any longer. This is, of course, no real solution, as we cannot escape this necessary confrontation.

Wakefulness is the key for our present situation. This is not a threat but a necessity. In such times we are not allowed to sleep. We are living in a state of emergency, hence we cannot lean back and think everything will be fine anyway. We are all needed, and we can only co-carry if we are awake.

It is not about understanding every smallest detail of what is happening, that you should not sleep at night any more in order to be always ready; the point is that we all need to make our light available. And we can do this only when we are present, when we inwardly understand what we are doing and what is needed from us humans. If we find ourselves, however, in the mode of sleep-consciousness, we simply cannot do this.

When I look at you incarnated people on earth, I have to regretfully say that the lights do not radiate yet. I said that I see all of you as lights, but sadly when I perceive the vast ocean of humans I see very few lights radiating freely.

And it is exactly this that serves those forces that wage their battle against life. They can play this gamble with us only until all the lights, and with these the whole ocean of humans, begin to radiate.

 Probably many people will now say: 'Can we not when it comes down to it simply look ahead and stop talking about this

dualistic world? Can we not just simply look forward and steer our strength in that direction?' But is it really that simple? Is it true that if we strengthen our focus strongly enough on the New, that it will become reality – and all that was, we simply allow to fade away?

Also this is a form of sleeping. When I look back on my journey from the visible to the invisible life, I can only say that it is not correct that one should simply look firmly ahead. This opportunity that we as human beings and souls have for evaluating our experiences is a huge gift – I do not mean analytically with our intellect but rather with our whole being. In this way we can learn from our past steps for our future steps. In every single moment we have the possibility to grow, change and expand ourselves through our experiences.

If we are only peering forwards we lose this possibility. The same counts for the collective situation as well.

The solution for our current situation does not lie in the future, but in the experiences we have already gathered and understood. Through this we gain strength that we can apply to the Now.

We cannot change the course of history and events without looking at them. We cannot change the circumstances if we do not look closely at them – and look at them as long as it takes to fathom their depths. This alone will enable us to take a new step.

It is an illusion to think that we can enter the New by inwardly leaving the Old behind. In a metaphor we can imagine the Old as a pile – it doesn't matter what it consists of – lying on top of the New.
As long as we have not shovelled this pile away we cannot reach the New. Of course it is important to have focus towards the New, else we would lack the strength, the wish and the right alignment to remove the pile. But such focus alone will not move the pile. It is time to work through it and transform it – which is only possible by becoming conscious. And the consciousness we can obtain only by understanding the Old more profoundly and by digesting it.

Remaining with the image of the pile I look once more to my journey as a soul: Of course I left this life with a pile on my shoulders – as all souls do and I am no exception. Since then I have been chewing on this pile, since then I have been grinding all my experiences; I am transforming, purifying and beginning to weave out of all of this something New. I am continuously spinning golden threads out of it. This gold I can spin by transforming the pile I have brought along with me. This may appear like a superior art and alchemy, but in a way we all do it the whole time!

Humanity is at a turning point, where a complete change is necessary. We need this turning point, as we have reached an absolute endpoint, the end of an epoch on this level. This is very similar to what I explained regards the journey of the soul after the crossing. It means we have reached the point at which we can and should spin this pile into gold. As already said, this is only possible with profound consciousness, with a clear presence, with wakefulness and readiness.

As humanity we can collapse under the weight of this pile if we continue to sleep and only dream of the New. Or we collect ourselves, get a grip on ourselves, pull our last strength together, and spin the pile into gold and weave something New. This demands of us that we WAKE UP and consciously confront what is happening right now, and out of all that we have experienced as humanity find the strength for this change.

As human beings we are too conscious to just leave this pile behind – no matter what it is made of – in order to begin something New somewhere else. It would not bring us the growth that we need for the New.

We are preparing ourselves for the next, higher level. For this we of course need a higher and wider consciousness – this we have to acquire by our own effort, plain and simple. We obviously do not possess this consciousness yet. We are on the path to this new level of consciousness and should avoid tackling it with our old way of thinking. Nothing is being given, everything has to be strenuously worked for.

Everything we experience and have experienced, personally and collectively

– here I do not mean just pleasant happenings, but even more so the challenging karmic legacies – we need to face them at some point, bring them into consciousness in order to be able to work through them inwardly, to transform them, to release them and in this way spin them into gold.

This is exactly what we as humanity are doing right now. We are confronting old entanglements, old shadows and patterns of abuse of life and all other patterns in which we have been caught up in multiple ways in the last 2000 years. This time, though, we do it to reach the turning point.

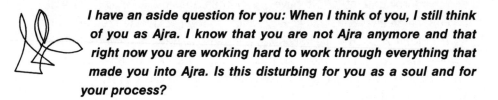

I have an aside question for you: When I think of you, I still think of you as Ajra. I know that you are not Ajra anymore and that right now you are working hard to work through everything that made you into Ajra. Is this disturbing for you as a soul and for your process?

There is a difference, whether one is conscious of all that we just talked about or not. If you were to limit me with my name to what I was as the human being, Ajra, and put me into a certain 'box', it would indeed disturb me. Moreover it would influence and limit our relationship very much. But because you know who, how and where I am now, it does not disturb me at all.

It is very confining, particularly when close persons cannot let go of us, if after many years they still cling to the image, appearance and all that once was. The sphere in which one can encounter one another becomes inevitably smaller, narrower.

I cannot entertain human relationships any longer, nor offer such to anyone, but I can encounter everyone as a soul. This is an exchange of a different kind, another form of contact, which however is no less intense. I can no longer give what I was as Ajra, but as soul I can offer much more.

If we manage together to leave our story as incarnated beings behind us and to touch one another from soul to soul, a completely new dimension can open up for both of us.

For most people this signifies a practice, a certain labour and even an inner overcoming. I rejoice GREATLY in every single person, who is ready to rise to this level and build this new relationship with me.

Then I am still allowed to say Ajra to you?

Yes, you are, because you leave me free, you see my width and understand it independently of my former presence.

I thank you. So, we were at a very current topic. What is in this case the gold we are spinning as humanity from out of the pile? Is it our wisdom, our knowledge about life? What is the gold that we need for our present process as humanity?

As already said, we find ourselves at a decisive, epochal moment in our human development. We are engaged in preparing a synopsis of the entire development of the last phase at the end of which we are arriving right now. The gold we are spinning is this synopsis.

At the same time we can understand the current condensed situation in the world as the synopsis of all that humanity has lived through over many thousands of years. As individual beings and souls we have already learned, practised, transformed and grown much through this –every individual has gone through many personal trials and tribulations. Together and each on one's own, we arrive now at the point when we 'take stock' and move into something New. What do we take along? What do we individually and collectively as humanity take along? What is the deep knowledge about ourselves and about us as humanity?

To be able to answer these questions, and especially to find the deep answers, we are currently travelling through this condensed phase. Expressed again in a picture: it is like a thesis at the end of our studies, which deals with the synthesis of our entire collated knowledge, or it is like an exam for which we prepare for many months.

To manage this synthesis of our consciousness, who we are as human beings, what constitutes our light and wherefore we let it shine, we 'need' an eye of a needle, through which we cannot pass so easily.

But we cannot achieve this synopsis in deep sleep, nor spin our gold; hence we need a booming wake-up call. First of all we need to recognise in what a decisive situation we find ourselves – not only how critical this is for humanity, but also what is threatening us, what it is that throws the spanner in the works in order to make us fail on our path of development.

Actually I myself do not really want to believe this to be true. Unfortunately, though, at the moment we are not only not spinning the pile into gold, no, we are making the pile grow even larger. Instead of collecting ourselves, focusing inwardly on what is at stake, we are so strongly alienated from ourselves and life that we are losing ourselves even further. In spite of all this I still remain optimistic and know we will manage this. But when one is in a position to observe the situation as I can, it does indeed look alarming.

Then help us, please. Give us clear references for where and how we can begin. What can we change, what can we do, how can we influence this huge event, which we are indeed all a part of? What is the personal step we can take to begin spinning the gold?

As you said, many, or I hardly dare to say it, most are still sleeping – what, however, can those do who are awake or waking up to this? What is our part? What is the call to us as souls?

Some things I have already mentioned, but I will attempt to be more concrete and give some further images.

If we as souls, as humanity, face something akin to a dying process

– of course not on the physical level – we need to inwardly prepare for this. I can say from my own experience what happens to a person in this process – from this then we will also be able to understand the current task more clearly.

For a personal transition from one dimension to another, the main task is to withdraw from your own physical presence in such a manner that we do not lose our true being-ness.

This means to let go of all attachments, all imagination, all expectations of yourself, of life and to free yourself from your own projections and those of your surroundings. This does not happen through the oft-quoted 'letting go', but on the contrary by condensing all of that which we are as being in our inner core.

Of course we spend our whole life considering the question of who we truly are, but now at this threshold we are confronted with this question in a different way. Let us not forget that as human beings we experience during the process of dying an intensity that we are not familiar with in life. The very best is being pressed out of us – the nectar of life.

In this moment there is only the pure life – there are no explanations, no excuses, no insignificant questions, no delusions, no obscure words, if as a soul we wish to progress with a more enlightened consciousness. There are of course also souls who seek to withdraw from this confrontation with the truth and do withdraw, but in doing so they will miss the most crucial moment of their life.

As an analogy one could say: Someone composes a great text but consciously omits the most beautiful and most important part. What meaning would such a text have then? What sense is there in life, if at the moment where we can experience and gain the best of ourselves, we withdraw from the confrontation with ourselves and with life.

In this moment every soul knows what, who and why she is – everything else falls away, the core alone remains. In such a moment we as souls have the chance and privilege to experience uniquely the clearest, deepest imprint of our soul.

No matter how consciously we have lived our lives, no matter on which side of life we chose to stand, no matter what kind of lies we might have followed – if in this instant we succeed as soul in gathering our strength to choose the naked truth, then we will experience our pure essence. And this is crucial for the further process of the transition because it depends precisely on this how far we can then spin our gold.

Our soul is now freed from the specific tasks of this particular life and returns to her core. At this moment the true maturity of the soul shows itself, all that she has truly learned in life.

The accumulated burden does not just disappear – for this the soul needs a longer journey still. But the purpose she had taken up through this specific role in life has been dissolved.

Depending on the learning process and consequently the task the soul has taken on, it can be an enormous liberation and relief when she does not have to play this role any longer.

In an image I could describe this feeling in the following way: The tightest garment that has been restraining the soul's width and breadth in this incarnated life is now being shed. Through further processes many more garments that are too tight will come to light, allowing the soul to gradually shed them step by step.

How can we recognise our current situation in the above process? We are finding ourselves at a rather similar junction: thus both personally and collectively as humanity we are being faced with a similar process. If we are conscious of this, we can prepare ourselves. We can inwardly look at our entanglements, habits, ideas, projections in regard to ourselves and to life right now, to first of all become aware that they are there and open ourselves inwardly for the next step, and most of all that we gather the strength to meet this reality.

As humanity we are still far from such an attitude to life. It seems rather that we need more severe confrontations and challenges. And yet again it is about nothing less than returning to the essence of who we are as humanity.

What can everyone contribute concretely? For both the personal and collective level it is crucial that the process becomes more fluid, fruitful and clear once the human being is inwardly ready for this emergence and does not attempt to withdraw anymore. Then the soul is free to make the first step towards her new birthing.

Then follows the big task for every single incarnated human being, to step by step detach from the arch of development he has accomplished over several thousand years.

How does one do that? It suffices to begin in the current life and to straighten out everything that is unsolved, all that is not worked through, all that oppresses – to look at, to clarify, to purify and therewith to let one's light shine ever clearer.

I know this is nothing new, but obviously nothing new can come unless we have digested the old.

Most important though is to remain loyal to both yourself and life! The danger that we lose ourselves as humanity is now more present than ever – that is why every human being who upholds and promotes the light and the true life is important and worth gold.

When we see clearly through the fog of mainstream reporting and news, the situation we find ourselves in as humanity looks grey and often truly hopeless. It is difficult to comprehend what is really happening and not always easy to keep one's confidence and trust in the course of events. Are we humans strong and lucid enough to pass through this dark tunnel? What helps us to stay awake and to actively support this process of transformation? What helps us to stay confident that the good within us will win through?

We as humanity have an eminently important role in the earth evolution, hence the spirit world won't leave us hanging. At some point though the emergency break will be pulled if it is not possible to get through this process unharmed in any other way. We are under divine protection and should never forget this. It won't be allowed that as humanity we lose our power, our true presence. This must not and will not come to pass.

For this we, the invisible part of humankind, are also here. We likewise will put in our veto, if humanity threatens to fall into the abyss, rather than letting it leap into it. All this is also about us – it is our decision and evolution as well, not only yours.

As humanity we have truly come into a very dense spiritual obscurity, which has never happened like this before. When looking onto humanity, as I am able to do right now, it is incomprehensible and unimaginable.

Tragically we as humanity are a part of the earth that is not even connected to the earth any longer. We are a part of the cosmos, but such a part that does not even know how to belong to the cosmos. Never before have we been both so un-grounded as well as non-connected to the spiritual dimensions as humanity. There have been phases, when the one might have been more pronounced and the other less visible – but that both connections are simultaneously so compromised and almost unattainable – this is entirely new.

I don't mean to say that one cannot have this connection, but for most people it is neither important nor necessary because they don't even know they could have this connection.

This denotes the fog and the degree of disintegration – everything is so far removed that we do not even notice what is missing, that there is something that is not only crucial but actually a part of us.

If I am part of the earth, the earth likewise is part of me. If I am part of the cosmos, the cosmos is part of me. If I am a spiritual being, then the spirit world is also part of me. If I am part of the divine, then the divine is also part of me!

When I look at you humans on earth, I cannot behold this anymore. This consciousness is lost to you, and it is just this fact that invariably gives you the feeling of being lost.

What does this portend for us humans?

You have lost your own thread of life.

It has gone too far. Looking at humanity from our spiritual perspective, we can say: much can be tolerated, but if the meaning of life is being forgotten, if your deeds do not serve life any longer but serve only the deeds themselves, when for example science purely serves science and not the evolving of humankind and the understanding of life, then it does not serve life any longer but step by step begins to work against life – at some point it will serve absurdity instead of sense, pure self-fulfilment in place of the fruition of life. Do you know what I mean?

Everything seems to be more and more about what is inconsequential and irrelevant – this is what produces the fog. You are obscuring yourselves evermore.

How do you reckon most people would respond to the question, what they wish from life? Most likely they would say that they long for a quiet, comfortable, rich and carefree life. But where is the content? The essence? Where is the participation in life, the creativity, where can we find the inner striving for inner growth? Where is the divine spark? Where does the consciousness dwell that we are all together serving something divine?

Here is where you can see so abundantly clearly our 'being lost'. And one of course can't but be lost when this orientation is missing.

We all know situations, phases, moments in life, when we neither sense nor see the meaning of our own life – this feeling that we are useless, not valuable, that it would make no difference whether we were there or not. In such a moment we are not capable of seeing ourselves in the larger context. We lose the greater picture of ourselves as soul, hence we are lost.

Transferring this kind of condition onto mankind, we can see where we stand. We personally become depressed if we remain in such a hole for too long. We can say the exact same thing as regards humanity. For too long now humanity has been stuck with this feeling of futility and has now truly lost all knowledge of its task.

Comparing this once more with our personal condition: if we feel lost in life, we do not have any longer the strength to forge a connection with our spiritual companions and therewith to seek support – we are so lost we won't even have an idea for how to do this. When we do not feel well inwardly, we won't have the idea to use an exercise to ground ourselves again, to get again in tune with the breath of the earth, to centre ourselves again within the earth. No, we prefer in this instance to stay lost and no longer see what would help us, or we even forget that the earth is there.

The same holds true for us as humanity. We have fallen so deep into this state of being lost, that we don't know anymore that we are lost – we are so deeply depressed that we do not know any longer we are depressed. Why should we change anything when we believe that our condition is normal?

Hence the most important thing now is that we as humanity first of all grasp the situation in which we find ourselves; that we realise how serious the situation is and also that we need to act immediately, otherwise it will really be too late at some point.
And for this we need a really strong shake up, otherwise we won't wake up. And if we don't wake up now we won't be lucid enough to catch up, to be part of this major transformation.

What can we individually do for this fog to lift? Or even better: what can we do, that we notice that we are muffled by this fog – that we are weakened, that we are not standing in our own inner strength? What could be our own personal contribution?

Most important is to stop viewing life as a flat, three-dimensional reality. Life happens simultaneously on multiple levels. That which you perceive as the true life – the physical sphere, which you perceive with your eyes – is only one of them.
How would we be able to recognise what a photograph portrays, if we were seeing just part of it or merely a few pixels?

Life does not run linear or just in one direction. The timeframe exists purely on the physical material level. It is known that the etheric stream of a river, which flows in the opposite direction to the current, is in reality stronger than the one flowing with the current. The same holds true for life.

The incarnated part of life as you experience it runs indeed from birth to death. But the real event is not tied to this direction of flow; this is why you as souls are constantly travelling here and there. We wonder why we are dreaming something, or why we think at particular moments of something that has happened a long time ago, why images arise that we cannot place.

If your human intellect would not constantly control things and you were freer, you might realise so much more. Sadly you are missing far too much of what is happening to you.

True, it is important to be present in the here and now, because only then you can achieve something in the material world in your incarnated human form. What is not true though is that you shouldn't at the same time travel inwardly parallel to this. As souls we need this freedom of travel because we are so much more than what we embody now as incarnated humans.

For each single incarnation we design a specific task, seek out a theme and enter into a concrete role. This we do not choose though according to whim and mood but according to the experiences we need as humans and souls, and which tasks from our experiences in former incarnations we still need to settle, to strengthen, to repeat or to pursue further.

In order to be able to transfer, to connect to and to continue the work with these experiences from previous lives we as souls need the opportunity to ever and again return to the feelings from before. Not to hold on to them, nor to get caught up with them but rather to be able to move on.

At the same time we need as incarnated souls access to our vision for the future, otherwise we could not follow our inner alignment and compass. As souls we have a deep knowing of our intentions and hence direction in life – for this though we need the freedom to again and again travel in this direction so that we can pursue the path leading to our goal.

Were we to be only in the here and now as incarnated souls, we would be lost. Some argue the opposite: you will lose yourself if you spend too much time with the past and future. This holds true for our daydreams, which we produce with our intellect, not so for our soul-movements, which are essential in order for her to expand her being.

Can you imagine how differently we would view one another as humans, how different education, schooling and life would be if we were conscious of this?

As incarnated souls we do indeed live a particular life, which at this moment is the main happening – simultaneously, however, the soul is under way on different levels as well.

In the process of incarnating we do have to block out parts of this happening and push them into our unconscious – because it would be too much for a human being to experience all components of the whole large picture equally strongly. As soul though we do need access to it and can only build this up when we are conscious that there are further parts to the picture than what we are seeing right now.

Were we to see the entire picture, we would get confused; if on the other hand we focus on too small a section, we would be lost because we as souls couldn't orientate ourselves any longer. The logical consequence is that we sleep through life. As souls we fall asleep, because otherwise we would be strangulated, cut off from the essential and therewith within our tiny capsule lost in the immense universe.

Translated into an image: it is similar to screening the earth off from the larger happening of the universe. How could the earth function at all if separated from the other planets, stars and life upon these? Where would she get her strength from and how would she orientate herself? And what, as further example, would happen to us humans on earth?

 In the best-case scenario we think that we return to our past only to retrieve information for this life or to clarify something. I say 'best case scenario', because most people won't even

consider this necessary or possible – for most people the personal story begins with their birth here on earth.
We only see the past as a storage of information, as a foundation for this life. However, if I understand rightly, our past is in actual fact an existing level, which not only was but still is part of our life.
Aren't we then living in absolute chaos? How does this look for/to you?

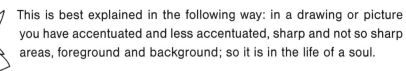

This is best explained in the following way: in a drawing or picture you have accentuated and less accentuated, sharp and not so sharp areas, foreground and background; so it is in the life of a soul.

Whilst observing you right now, I see in the foreground the strength which you live right now as a human being, what you incarnate, what you manifest, what you are as human being. But in the background I also see what you do not currently manifest, what you carry within you as soul, what you have lived already and also what you will live in the future – your as yet not incarnated potential. This is for me like a multidimensional image that I can contemplate. Only as a whole does it give me a feeling of who and what you are as a soul.

You are strongly, even exclusively focused on what you are as human beings right now, and through this lose more and more the ability to recognise who you are as souls. You encounter one another merely as human beings and lose the expansiveness of your soul.

If I meet a person solely as a human being and not also as a soul, again I reduce her/him to only a small portion of the whole larger picture. I won't perceive who this person is as a soul, nor who I am as a soul.
When I meet someone purely in her/his current human form, I miss the opportunity to encounter her/him fully. I remain on a level that cannot impart enough of this person to me so that I could truly touch her/him as a soul.

Do you understand? We meet people who are important for us on our current journey. They are important to us because we have something to do with each other as souls – because we have either made an arrangement as souls or because we need to share something from a previous life or even to clarify something. If during this encounter we remain purely on the human level, the danger is great that we miss the meaning of this encounter with the other soul.

It is like multiple registers that we open or do not open. If we do not open them they remain shut. Simple logic. If a channel is blocked, nothing can flow through it. Staying with our encounter on just the one level, we may if lucky experience unconsciously further levels or simply nothing. At least if we allow this exchange on other levels to enter our unconscious, we will be able at a later stage to take it up, else it will be lost to us.

To see everything, sense everything, to remember everything would obviously be too much for you and us; it is not too much, however, if we have the openness and a consciousness for it. It will not give us less but on the contrary a stronger orientation, a clear inner calm and a tangible certainty that we are being carried.
If we decide for such an image of life that flows simultaneously in various directions and dimensions, then we are not isolated any longer within our small personal space, but with this space become a stronger part of the greater whole. This gives our life entirely new dimensions. To this end the consciousness and preparedness suffice, more we do not need. Everything else will fall into place. We simply exchange the stage of life in which we are used to acting – suddenly it is our private little room no longer, but the large stage, the multidimensional world.

When life acquires a larger dimension, then human life becomes a small part of the large circle. When I am invisible to you, or as you say 'dead', this does not mean that I am no longer part of life. I do not live less intensely here than when and how I lived my life on earth. The developmental steps are no smaller than the ones I made in my incarnated life. My presence is no weaker than the one I possessed as Ajra.
Why then am I in your understanding not an equal part to you incarnated human beings in life?

Why is the invisible part of life not seen, or even being ignored? Why is there so much fear in connection with dying? Why do you remember the currently invisible souls only in connection with the flowers on the cemetery when they are nevertheless an equal part of life? Why can't we jointly ensoul, enliven and form this human soul sphere?

The answer is simple: because a large blanket of manipulation is spread across all this, which uses our fears to keep us small.

It is time that we finally awaken!

I do sense your pain that we as humanity are separated from you, that we visible human beings neglect you invisible human souls, that we forget you and give you no space in our lives. I sense your frustration and would gladly present the opportunity here for you to give us a better understanding of how the life after life looks like. Can you elucidate some more how your presence is in this condition?
What is helpful for us as incarnated souls so that we finally open our inner eyes and ears to you non-incarnated souls? How do we learn to listen and how can we let you participate differently?

The most important would be to take our sphere into your consciousness. We are not able to directly influence physical matter after we have definitively separated from the physical body, hence it is difficult for us to enter into your world if you don't open yourselves for this.

Though we are indeed engaged in our own processes, nevertheless we are an important part of the whole of the human community – and would gladly be a much more active part thereof.

We do live, although we have no physical body; we live although you cannot see us. We are indeed invisible but then we have an enlarged perspective.
It is not firstly about giving you advices and wishing to guide you, or that you only turn to us when you need our help and support, but rather that you allow us to become part of life – that we live together. Then all that we have described will develop surely and naturally.

It may sound unusual: "Now we should live together with the dead, invite them in instead of leaving them to rest." We are not dead, we just don't have a physical body, we are not incarnated as you are right now, we have no loud voices, but we are present and we live!

The biggest hindrance is that as humanity we have excluded the whole of the spiritual dimension, that we do not take this seriously in mainstream any longer – it has no weight anymore. In this way the invisible realm of the non-incarnated souls has also been devaluated and declared unreachable. Hence it is only accessible for dreamers, esotericists and people who one can't take seriously. The natural communication with the non-incarnated souls has been labelled as 'talking with the deceased' and so the natural exchange has been taken from us.
At present incarnated people behave as if they will remain forever on the physical side, never to enter this other side.

We can give so much to each other and enrich one another. The image of death and of the life-after-life would fundamentally change if we were reunited.

You have no need to see me to be in contact with me; you only need to know that I am there – and then I will be there. That is what is so beautiful: we do not need to travel to visit each other, we can be together anytime and anywhere.
The most important thing in this is the openness and consciousness.

The less you try to create ideas for how this communication should unfold, the easier it will be to find a possible exchange. To perceive us is even simpler than, for example, to sense an angel presence or an elemental being, because on one level we are indeed one – all of humankind is part of the human ocean.

Maybe I will give a few more images of how our soul existence is after having left our corporeal home.
The idea that we are still wandering around in the same houses, rooms as in life and wish to sleep in the same beds and hence harass the people, is not true. This only happens in situations where a soul cannot realise that she

has left the physical world. This can also happen when during the process of dying something important to the person has not been worked through and consequently she is still as if caught in the material world. But even then it mostly does not apply to the whole of the soul, only to those parts that are still seemingly caught in life. There are examples where the burden on the soul is too heavy and therefore the soul cannot let go. If added to this those bereaved are holding on to the soul, hindering the process of detaching, the soul cannot cast off the thread of light connecting her to matter and she won't be able to release herself from the physical.

In the usual course of events the soul after her delivery – I use here consciously the same word that you use for the birth of a child, as this is indeed a birth – is freed from her human form and with this also from space-restrictions. This is, of course, a process that does not happen instantly with the last breath.

As I said earlier, the soul remains for a while near the material world and, if possible, near her 'own' body, near her fellow human beings and hence also in the spaces she lived in. But slowly this bond becomes weaker; for the soul within her process it becomes at some point rather disturbing, and because of this she separates fully from the earthly-material sphere.

If I take myself as an example: in my last incarnated life I was Ajra, have lived my role as a mother, healer, wife, daughter, sister etc. I have lived and worked in several places and died in Sempas, my last place of residence. In my process of transformation – the process of dying – I have let go of all those roles, I dissolved as Ajra and all my places of residence lost their importance for me.

It does not mean, however, that I have lost all of this; indeed, they have left deep traces within me, but have become like vessels out of which my soul can no longer be nourished. That's why I have shed them. Why should I hold on to them any longer? That which I have learned through my life on earth and have gained from it, how I have grown through it and been formed by it, all this has of course remained as trace within me, but as soul I have no need of these roles anymore to advance further, so I could relinquish them.

Because I am no longer tied to matter, I have no physical or any other roots. The only rootedness I need right now is the anchoring within my own being. I am not scattered throughout the all-being-ness, but rather am as close to my own being as I could never be in my earthly life. This is now also my main task. I centre and condense my essence and furthermore cleanse all that I have gathered in my last life. I spin all experiences into gold.

This is the true time of growth for the soul – in our life as humans in physical matter, we are so occupied and consumed by our circumstances, influences, insights, experiences and all the events around and within us, that there is much that we do not allow fully to come close to us, that we swallow many a thing undigested/partly chewed, that there is much we do not see; even though as souls we may be strongly touched by it, we miss noticing many things on the visible level and yet it manifests itself in our etheric body.

In the phase that I find myself in right now as soul, much of this becomes my nourishment, because I work through it. I am engaged in the soul's harvest. And this lasts a long time – one really can't imagine how long a soul can feast on her experiences on earth.

When I listen to you I get the impression that the transition process of dying is actually a very intense event for the soul; it is not about suffering, goodbyes or loss. Why though do we humans associate it exactly with this? And in reality we do see many people suffering when they are dying. Why?

As humans we always have/are in pain when something is ending, no matter what. Due to the fact that throughout our whole life we nurture this limited image of death, that our own experience of previous lives is lost for most and we do not hold the multi-dimensional image of life in our consciousness, we live our whole life with the expectation, vision and conviction that at the end we will suffer and grieve on leaving this life.

Maybe I need to add: the process of dying itself is a highlight of life; what is difficult, however, is the process before, above all because we do not know the truth about the life after life.

By this I mean: if you were still fully standing in life as I was then and become seriously ill, for example, and have to face the inner battle of this decision. The thought of having to leave the children, loving people, the life and all your acquaintances around you is painful, and it pains every human being. The beginning of this process of releasing from the body and matter is not easy either, again in many different respects, because as civilisation we do not have images or concepts for this crossing rooted within us.

Only when we lose more and more power as human beings and through this gain ever more as soul does this process become as a rule easier. Then we can let go: we have arrived at the threshold.

This feeling that we are losing the physical matter that has carried us until now, brings with it much fear. Matter symbolises and gives us security in life. As human beings we tend to equate physical matter with our physical body, most people even with their own I – with their own presence. And this thought that in dying we not only lose our physical body but our whole being, that we lose everything, inevitably makes the end of life so frightening. If only we knew that through this transition we indeed come again closer to our true I, then death would be much kinder and simpler.

If I now attempt to caricature this a bit I could say, dying is seen as a battle – a battle with death. In this image we namely lose everything that we have, even all that we are. Obviously, we try to defend ourselves against this and attempt to push death away from us as long as possible.

Such souls that have a more intimate relation to the invisible spheres of life and hence to the spiritual dimensions, will arrive sooner at the stage where the letting go is happening and hence also sooner at the real transition. In contrast, for those people who have lost the true connection to their own soul and with this also to the whole of the spiritual panoply of life, it will be more arduous to come to an inner peace. They do everything to save themselves, to paddle back and do not realise: if they battle against death, they inevitably battle at the same time against life. This of course does not ease the process, but only impedes and prolongs it further.

Then the suffering in reality comes like a deliverance for the soul, as the human being is almost being forced to let go.

Is that the moment of the process in which we would say from our perspective: she has lost the will to fight or he has given up?

Yes, exactly. It does not mean, though, that one has lost the strength to fight, that one has given up, but the human being has at last come to such inner peace that s/he is able to let go. Now the soul can take on the guiding of the process.

With this the liberating part of the process of dying begins.

Here maybe yet another aspect. In the moment that a person is confronted with her/his own death – usually due to a severe illness or an accident – s/he is inevitably confronted with the course of her/his own life. Questions arise, as for example: Who am I? What have I achieved in my life? What has been my task? What have I brought into this life with my being? And connected to this the fear arises that I might not have achieved what I had set out to do as a soul.

If we have not been contented with ourselves in this life, to our perception feel we have not done enough, the confrontation with the physical ending of life becomes more challenging and more painful.

If we have a very negative image of ourselves, it not only slows and blocks us in this life but also very strongly during our passage to the non-material life. For people who have poor self-confidence, who do not value and love themselves sufficiently, it is painful to leave life. They sense themselves too little and do not realise how much they have experienced, accomplished and moved. Their picture of their own life is incomplete and therewith the prospect of having to leave this life is accompanied with a feeling of loss and frustration. The path for such people is a longer one for arriving at the point of being ready to let go. For many then this phase can last not just months but years.

Will all souls, once they have made the decision to leave and been able to inwardly let go of the material world, experience how liberating and beautiful this crossing is?

Unfortunately, these days we interfere too often with this process by way of our highly developed medicines. People are being resuscitated, given artificial respiration, filled up with drugs and far too often disrupted in their natural passage of dying. Depending on how the path proceeds, what the human being and her/his soul have to go through, all this will be part of their own journey.

Due to this the opportunity to live consciously through this crucial process is sadly often taken away from the soul. Which does not necessarily mean that the soul can't or won't experience it. But her experience of it will be dampened, and she will have to make up for some of it in the further course of the process.

We can definitely compare the process of dying with the process of birth. The birth is for a soul the entry into life and contains in a sense the whole of life. The exact same can be said about the birth into the invisible phase of life – the dying of the physical body. It is the entry into the etheric sphere and opens the gate for the soul.

As much as the birth is a reflection of life, so is the dying a reflection of the life-after-life. It influences life in both directions – the life and the life-after-life.

The general disconnect from the life-after-life and therewith from the meaning of the process of dying has sadly strongly reduced the festive mood around dying. From the medical point of view all revolves around trying to save the person, without being able to perceive that the soul is following an inner path when bidding goodbye to the physical life. Those people grieving for the dying person are often solely occupied with their own sorrow about the loss and with their fear and sympathy for the person who is departing.

In this way we regrettably so often miss the magnificence, the beauty, the essence of this process. Instead of being part of this process, which for those present is also perceptible and moving, we are just standing by or are even inwardly absent.

How is it with those human beings who die unexpectedly due to an accident or heart attack – do they experience a somewhat shortened version of the whole process? They cannot really inwardly prepare themselves. How does the soul experience this?

Just as the whole of life is a process of learning, so also is this transition of the soul quite clearly chosen by this soul, depending on what kind of experiences she needs for her growth and depending on how her life's journey has proceeded.

It is impossible to generalise, as it is really individual, why a soul chooses such a sudden passing. Here are a few more thoughts about this.

There are souls who on earth will exhaust all their life's potential, remain on earth up to a ripe old age and so make the most of a human being's full life cycle and then die a so-called natural death. This does not automatically mean that they human beings are prepared to go. Even when the dying is part of the natural process, it is possible that the soul nonetheless is not ready to let go and is quite lost throughout the process of dying.

As already indicated, a person can be warned by way of a severe illness that as an incarnated soul s/he needs a fundamental change, because s/he has deviated from her intended path.
Such an illness also offers the opportunity to begin an entirely new life within this same life.

Some souls, though, pull the emergency break and do not give the person the opportunity for an extensive change – here the emergency exit is the variant of the unexpected death.

Another reason for the soul to pull the emergency break could also be the necessity of the experience itself – the soul is being catapulted out of life, and this without a conscious decision for this, without experiencing a slow process of letting go. She is therewith challenged to collect herself much more succinctly and to translate the earthly existence more condensed into the etheric. In this case only the essential and pivotal of the whole of her life will be 'taken along' for the soul. Here the soul experiences a compressed transition, which offers a great potential for learning.

Important to add here is that often in such a scenario the soul will nevertheless have unconsciously been preparing for this departure during her lifetime.

Then there is such a way of leaving in which the human being decides to take her/his own life. What happens to the soul in this case? At present there is much discussion in society on whether one should allow this medically. One philosophises on the theme of euthanasia, but how does this look from your perspective?

This is a question that I cannot answer briefly; too much else relates to this.

As you have already indicated, in most cases it is the decision of the incarnated person and not the soul. I say mostly, as there are also souls who need such an experience as human being and as a soul for their own development. But this is extremely rare.

A person reaches the edge of the abyss and does not see any possibility to progress, to move on. This only shows that this person has alienated her/himself from their soul, because the soul would always find a solution for progressing further. The soul knows her life's plan, always sees a step ahead and hence cannot lose herself – the human being can lose the thread of life, but not so the soul!

This may possibly sound for some shallow and old-fashioned, but whether it pleases us or not, it is like this, that we do learn our profoundest lessons as human beings and souls precisely when we are not so well, when we wrestle with ourselves, when we feel helpless, clueless and useless – and therewith meaningless. Those are such experiences and processes through which we touch on our deepest karmic points, wounds and themes. Karmic questions arise in such phases, so that we can confront ourselves with them, with the opportunity given to us to heal and transform them.

These are the darkest phases in all of our lives – every human being travels through one or more such phases, and for some it is even a permanent state of affairs throughout their whole life.

It does not help trying to escape from these confrontations, even if everyone would rather like to do that. Every human being arrives during such periods at least once at the point where s/he wishes to pull the emergency break, to once and for all leave the agonising life situation behind and to end this challenging incarnation.

If we know of the cyclic and eternal nature of the soul and know that we souls, precisely for this reason, travel through different incarnations to learn, to practice, to heal and to transform, then we also understand that again and again the soul has to pass through the eye of the needle in order to more deeply purify herself , to confront herself more thoroughly with herself, to comprehend more distinctly her own being, to peel away the layers as to what matters in life and in so doing to enter more fully into life.
We cannot evade such processes. Therefore the decision to end one's life is very short-sighted – which may offer a short-term rescue and maybe helps in that moment to extricate oneself out of an unbearable situation, but in the long term it brings neither a solution nor a clarification and certainly no improvement. As souls and also as humans we cannot withdraw from our life-themes, life-confrontations and life experiences. Self-evidently we will be presented with the same theme in our next incarnation and quite possibly not in a simpler form but rather in an even more difficult one. This does not occur in order to punish the soul, but because now the situation for the soul is even more involved, confused and knotted.

Those who know how to knit will understand this metaphor well: one is knitting something and then putting it aside, to pick it up again later. And there is a significant difference whether you will find the started project still on the needles or if they have slid off them in the meantime. In the first scenario you can start knitting straight away, in the second one will need first a lot of time, nerves and patience, to return all the stitches to the needle – a troublesome job, which however does not present any result as yet, but only serves being able to start.

It is similar for a soul who has been catapulted out of life due to an emergency reaction – she will need a lot of strength, a lot of time and a lot of patience to find herself again, to compose herself, to get back to the point where she is in a position to continue with the real soul-work.

Even if it is sometimes totally intolerable in life, with no improvement in sight, even if it is utterly dark and there are enough reasons to despair, one should under no circumstances throw away one's life. Not only is it unhelpful in the long run but it does bring us into even deeper distress. We can't raise this strongly enough to all our awareness.

We should know that exactly these low points, even if they might last a whole incarnation, advance us far as souls, because we can really 'crack' difficult karmic images, memories, burdens and pains and can free ourselves enormously for the long term.
As soul we will be richly rewarded, if we manage to persevere and carry through with life, even if we momentarily do not see any chance that the situation might improve. We can also clarify to ourselves that in such inner turmoil we are hardly in a position to see far enough ahead, to judge our true situation as a soul – often times we cannot see the light at the end of the tunnel, which doesn't mean it is not there though.

To give up in such a situation and take one's own life is the worst decision we could take. We all need to take note of this – it does not take us further, but instead throws us several steps backwards.

In contrast to a sudden and for the person unexpected death, in the case of a suicide the soul is not prepared for the crossing: she contracts so severely that she needs a long time to surface again from this state of shock. The soul quite often loses all orientation through a suicide, or she does not even notice that she has changed her state of being but continues to live with the assumption that she is still incarnated within the physical body. Even once she recovers from the shock, she will need a long time to find her own way again. Moreover, tragically, many of the experiences and memories gathered in life are lost to the soul – through the experienced shock she is no longer in a position to fall back on her treasure chest.

Though it may sound hard and dramatic, the soul may sometimes even need several incarnations to arrive back at the point in her development where she found herself as soul before. It shows what a drastic experience this is for the soul.

Also here there are of course exceptions and quite varying journeys, hence these are insights which by no means apply to everyone.

How is it with the so called chemical medical aids, which are supposed to help a person to 'free' her/himself from the torments of an incurable illness or agonising pains? What happens to the soul if she evades the natural process of dying, by means of such poisons as are being used nowadays in 'euthanasia'? How does the passage of the soul look like then?

All the previous answers also apply in this case, only that it is even more dramatic what this means for the soul.

An incurable illness is not a mistake on the path of a human being and her/his soul, nor a breakdown like with a car which needs repairing. A serious illness is part of the path which this soul has chosen, a precious stone for her truly individual mosaic which the soul will fashion in the course of her life.

As souls we cannot simply skip such an experience because this experience is much more important for the soul than we imagine.

Say a person is lying for months or even years motionless in bed, suffering perhaps terrible pain; this in no way means that during this time the soul does not actively experience, work through, prepare, transform and hence as a soul possibly make huge steps.

We view such situations too much purely from our human standpoint and think it does not make sense to continue living in such a condition.

Medicine is often very helpful, in some situations brilliant and a great blessing, but we should never give it 'general power of attorney', most decidedly not when we talk about dying. We forget too quickly that here we have an eternal soul, who is gathering experiences as a human being right now. It is not just about a purely mechanical and therewith merely physical body, which might in this instance really be sick, but it's about an active and living process of the human being and more importantly the soul.

One speaks of this innocently as 'assisting with dying', but what the soul experiences through this is far from harmless and farther still from being helpful. Yes, it will take away the pain and maybe even liberates the person in that moment, but the soul will have to pay dearly for this.

The body is being brutally snatched away from the soul, one could even say stolen. As already described, the soul contracts in a state of shock, but in this case the soul is literally being shattered. The poison causes a kind of explosion, which severs the soul abruptly and far too quickly from the body. It does not leave any time for the soul to first compose herself, as happens in the usual process of dying, but she is being atomised into the expanse of the all-being. Hereby she loses herself completely. The soul cannot turn within herself to find her own focus again but is shattered and as if disintegrated.

This is a true catastrophe for the soul – if only we knew what really happens to the soul, no one would decide for such a death. What from the outside seems maybe like a short-cut is actually for the soul an unbelievable detour. A long, extremely arduous and painful route. One cannot do any greater harm to the soul; it is worse than the most dreadful that a soul can experience in an incarnated life.

The soul experiences a veritable annihilation.

First she is as if cut up and lost. It needs a very long and onerous process until the soul realises at all what has happened to her. Only with a lot of help and support will she be able to master this step – without help she is just lost.
The soul will have to then gather herself together totally anew – it is as if the soul had to refashion herself. Like pieces of a puzzle, which she has to put together in the right way to allow herself to newly emerge. Thereby she not only loses a lot of strength, which she would otherwise have needed for

*This is how the space feels in which the process of dying
happens in a healthy way*

other important processes of development, but she also loses many pieces of the puzzle of her own being as well as crucial experiences of the last and even of former incarnations.

When I perceive how fragmented the soul becomes through this, I could truly despair of humankind. So much that is devastating is being done, covered up with embellishing slogans, manipulative phrases, which have nothing – NOTHING – to do with the true life. Rather much more with the complete opposite.

To harm a soul in her core so very much, to destroy, and at the same time without even knowing what one is doing to moreover be proud how one is 'easing' the dying for this person. I have to admit that I am lost for words – that it is possible for humankind to have strayed so far from life.

From a spiritual perspective such a way of dying is absolutely impossible, not allowed. PLEASE do prevent this wherever possible!!

In the same context I have another current theme, which does not only relate to the process of dying, but also to the life of a person. I would love to hear from you what kind of effect the Corona vaccination might have on the human being and on the soul. Unfortunately, there are already many reports of people dying after such a vaccination. Could you tell us something that could help us understand what we are dealing with here?

Life has been unassailable in its deepest layers, as long as human beings had not found a way to penetrate into the deepest kernel – on the physical level this means, as long as we had not learned to interfere with the script of our DNA. This namely is the point where the real danger begins, that life is being changed, manipulated and abused in the purest layers.

Everything that lives carries within it the divine breath, which gives life a foundation, shape and framework. This pure impulse is being held and protected within our cells, because it is essential to all living beings. When we lose this divine purity, we lose the direct access to our own nature, to our origin, to our being, to the creation of life.

We can change, twist, mutilate, distort, manipulate, exchange everything within and around us and we would continue to be who we are, AS LONG AS this purest divine script remains unchanged. If we sully this, however, we lose our very own foothold.
Expressed in an image, we could compare it with a simple temple structure which we rob of its central column – there is no more support and it must crumble.

The moment that we penetrate and change the purest divine script of our physical body, we have broken into the holy chamber of our being.

This whole campaign for the vaccinations sadly shows us how much we humans have removed ourselves from ourselves, from nature, from our creation and from the divine. Never before as humankind have we implemented such worldwide collective alienation. As humanity we are now truly standing in danger of destroying ourselves.

In many respects we have already lost ourselves quite extensively as humanity, but now we are really standing before a collective catastrophe. In this we are losing the divine thread that provides us with our fundamental orientation in life.

Many might now object and argue that it is impossible that, due to a simple vaccination, we could be so seriously injured and getting lost as human beings. If it were just a simple vaccination there wouldn't be a problem, but as this one has the capability and tendency to penetrate into the purest space of our existence, it is neither harmless nor innocent.

I do have to add though that not all humans will react in the same way, nor would the purest core be attacked within every individual. But already the possibility for this to happen is absolutely too much.

In the event this does happen, though, the physical body becomes so alien to the soul, so cold, unrecognisable and unreachable, that she would not be able any longer to enliven it. The separation between body and soul becomes such that all of a sudden the soul feels herself in her own body like in a prison. This is for life as well as in dying unbearable.

If it does come to this, life becomes a horror; also the consequences after dying are similar to how I have already described them in response to the former question.

We should become conscious of the following when we speak about this vaccination: This medium has not been created to help mankind but rather to push her into such distress, that she feels lost and therefore is prepared to follow a particular path of alienation.

As already said, one could not equate this with death, yet everyone should try to sense well what the true background is to this and whether one really wants to serve this intended scheme.

We humans are such pure carriers of life and the divine, that we must serve LIFE and only life.

[The following question was put to Ajra at a later point in time, when in some countries already two-thirds of the population or more had been vaccinated. It is inserted here to offer a follow-up perspective.]

Unfortunately, there has been no true and widespread education about the Corona vaccination, many people have not informed themselves about it, have not been interested in it and have believed that it is a help and medicine for humankind and have been vaccinated, not knowing what the consequences are. If the truth about the damage caused by this vaccination becomes more and more widespread, it is possible that many people will now realise that they have unwittingly taken part in a dangerous 'experiment'.
What can they do then? Are there ways in which they can still save themselves from this snare?

As a no longer incarnated soul, having a broader view, I can only shake my head. It is probably really difficult to see through when one is concretely incarnated in matter, and yet it is almost painful to see how many manipulations are not seen through.

Of course, current manipulations, including the current vaccination campaign, are very perfidious, targeted, and very exactly and meanly prepared, and yet I would expect more presence and alertness from humanity.

It will sound dramatic, but this vaccination is about a very simple decision: for or against life. If one decides for the vaccination and thus against the true power of life, then this is not a small decision, and so it is not so easy to change it. By this I do not mean that it is not possible, but the new decision for life should be not just 80% but 200%.

Of course, it is not about proving to any higher 'authorities' that you are serious this time, but rather that you need so much strength of decision to be stronger than the effect of this medication.

Maybe it will help if I describe how I see it from my perspective. As humans, we have an anchoring to the earth and cosmos that is visible to me, which allows us to exist in the multidimensional world. For example, the earth's magnetic field holds us on the physical plane, and the anchoring I'm talking about here holds us on the spiritual-soul plane. This is not only a connection to the power of the earth and the cosmos but is rather like a spiritual current and thus also exchange, which is very essential for us humans. Through this we humans are the connecting link between different dimensions, which is also the main role and sense of our existence. If we lose this, then we lose the basic soul orientation.

And the side effect of vaccination on the soul level is exactly the loss of this fine anchoring. What does this mean in concrete terms? Many people may not even notice this consciously, because they were already more or less alienated from themselves, from the earth, from the divine. But if you had this direct connection to other dimensions before, then it is drastically expressed in an image like when you suddenly disconnect the antenna when listening to the radio.

As humans we are physical beings, but we so often forget that we are much more spiritual beings. We are spiritual beings embodied in matter. This means that we are first at home in the spiritual worlds. We therefore need direct exchange with the spiritual dimensions in order to survive in matter at all. Do you understand what I mean?

We can live in matter only if we can continue to receive spiritual impulses and thus follow them.
If this direct thread is cut, then we are lost in matter. It is like a butterfly suddenly finding its way in water. This is a bit of an exaggeration, but without this connection we are thrown into matter that is unknown to us from our origin. I absolutely do not mean to say that the earth is foreign to us, but it is still a learning process for us as beings to be embodied in physical matter. We are only at home in the earth when we can feel the spiritual vastness.

Coming back to your question, it means that we must find and build our spiritual connection again after this externally caused disconnection. This sounds easy, but it is not at all in the given state because we by ourselves are not able and in the inner condition to do that.

The whole thing is a rowing back, which is never easy. Besides physical consequences, which of course should be looked at and treated in parallel, the soul consequences can only be overcome from an absolute conviction and inner commitment. As I said before, it is about a YES for life, and to turn such a deep-seated NO into a YES means an intense inner journey.
I would even dare to say that this correction is only possible if one is prepared to turn life and much of one's own personal life completely upside down. In this case, the soul must find its positioning completely anew and allow its own being to be created anew. It is not a matter of choosing a new personality, but of putting together anew the existing being and thus finding soul orientation again.

In simple words we could say that in this case the human being has to convince his own soul that he has really chosen life and wants to serve it out of deep conviction.
In any case, this is a process that one can hardly manage alone, without

the accompaniment and support of one's own fellow human beings and professional help.

If you cut a vein, you can't sew it back together on your own, so you can only reactivate this spiritual vein with the support of others.

Everything is possible and if you really decide inwardly, then of course there is a way forward in this case as well.

That is really intense, and the truly sad thing is that we have not the faintest idea of what we are creating. How can this be? How can it be that we humans have become so blind?

The dying is simultaneously the birth into the invisible dimensions and the spheres of the soul – it is as important or even more important than birth itself because we are returning home with the fruits of our life. And us? We have forgotten all this, we are no longer conscious of it and therewith ignorant about life.

What would be important for us to learn here?

The physical dying is neither death nor the end. The human being with her/his specific role, her/his personality, her/his tasks, her/his unique look and physical appearance is indeed no longer there, but the fruit of all of this moves on with the soul. Nothing is either forgotten or lost, much more remains than just the past, which we remember. It is still the living present that continues to live and is carried further by the soul.

The process of dying is a highly spiritual event and a holy deed. Life again pours itself into the immense being-ness – as a greatest gift the kernel is being given back to life like a ripe fruit. This is a celebration of life – and indeed of the purest life!

The soul can find herself again in the all-being, free herself and rest. She is close to the divine as never before. She is not only part of the divine and the divine of her, but she is one with the divine. This is the most supreme and purest condition of the soul, which is why the transition to this sphere is so important and significant.

If I exaggerate a little I could say, throughout our whole life the soul prepared itself for this transition. There is some truth in these words because the soul uses life to gather experiences, which she integrates into her own being after having left the physical life behind.

This transition, the now common handling of death, is the biggest split we human beings carry within our being, not only on the collective level but also quite personally. We are thereby separated from our ancestors, we have lost the connection to the non-incarnated souls, and we have closed ourselves off from the invisible spheres, dimensions and beings.

Due to the fact that we not only live this separation so clearly but declare it to be our only reality, it has power over us. It has turned into a veritable energetic barrier and partition. Humanity is immensely weakened by this. Not alone through this separation from the sphere of the non-incarnated souls, but also by shifting the spiritual dimensions and layers into the incomprehensible and thereby into a subordinate sphere, we have barred the direct access for ourselves.

Our relationship to dying is not only a maiming of life but also an inner limitation, which weakens us in our being and robs us in many respects of the most central in life – the joy of life and the freedom of our existence.

Life is a continuous circle, which exists due to it always revolving. It grows because it is constantly in a circling movement. It does not turn in the same place, but grows, expands and ascends ever higher. This circle we should not imagine flat – two-dimensional – but as a multi-dimensional, upright rising circle.

The birth out of the spiritual sphere into the physical realm is part of this circle in the same way as the birth out of the physical sphere into the spiritual realm is an important part of this circle of life.

When we now imagine this circle of life pictorially and add to it the tear, which has developed over a long period of time in our being around the point of dying, we can see and understand inwardly what this means for this circling river of life. This is the site where we lose most of our power as humanity – it is like a leaky point, like a hole in a vessel, through which precious life energy is continually being lost.

We do not go through the process of dying just once either in the personal or in the collective life cycle but arrive again and again as soul at this point of crossing on our eternal journey.

When viewed on the collective level it is even more disturbing because people die every moment of the day, which means that every moment new tears and crevices arise – there will always be more and more.

I do not tell you this because, observing from my so-called other side, I would wish to worry or punish you. No, I only wish to clarify with this image, how dramatic the consequences are of this 'not-understanding-of-death'. As humanity we are losing so very much through this. It deprives us of the opportunity to experience life as an eternal process.
We rob ourselves of the feeling that life is a sustaining vessel that gives us ground. Thus life unconsciously becomes an enemy, which takes everything from us during our dying. How then can we have trust in life?

It is indescribably important that we see life again as this vessel and allow ourselves to be carried. This would give us deep inner peace, contentment, serenity, joy and spontaneity.

When I observe you humans, I experience you in constant flight and alarm mode. This makes life incredibly stressful and draining of energy. Yet life should not be like this – this is by no means the normal condition. You have merely adopted this as your norm, but it is ever so far removed from the true life! But you do not even sense this any longer, because you have lost the feeling for this great carrying vessel of life and no longer see the constant flow of life.

Water does not lose itself when it evaporates from the liquid into the airy state of being, because the fundamental consciousness is present that it is a circling, that afterwards it will return again to its liquid state and then descend again back to earth.

This we can apply directly to the eternal circling of the soul – she likewise changes ever and again the state of her physical presence into the invisible sphere of the soul and from the land of the soul back to the physical presence.

In this process there is no end, no final passing away or dissolving.

Precisely this constant change gives us the chance to enter into the wonder and charm of life. Just imagine how boring it would be if we as souls were to stand in just one role in life for the whole of eternity? Isn't this idea unbearable? It would be like a prison.

That is true, it really hurts when I envisage this. But from where does the fear of death arise, if death is only a transition?

And this fear accompanies us not only in dying, but also during the other transition, the process of being born – not only the descending soul, but the whole environment senses fear, starting with the mother and the whole medical accompaniment. What is this fear, why do we succumb to it again and again? Can you say a bit more to this?

There are several aspects. However, let's first look at the most important one.

When we look at our spiritual connection to the divine, which is of course closely linked to how we view life, we can see very clearly that as humanity we have lived a very intimate, natural and healthily self-assured relationship to the spiritual dimensions and the divine, until the religious structures were forced upon us. Never mind whether that be the Christian, Islamic or Hindu-religion, they have convinced us to hand over our direct access to the divine to intermediary authorities. Therewith we have lost our very own key, our intimate connection. We have shut the door and hence the vast and unhindered view into the spiritual dimensions.

If we translate this into a simple image: we would receive water whenever we are thirsty, but the tap is so high up that we can't reach the water ourselves

Help for inwardly freeing oneself from the invisible seal or code

any more – so we have ended up in a dependency. We cannot get to the fountain by ourselves but with the help of an intermediary.

At this point and in the position we now find ourselves in, the great abuse of power begins.
Namely through this we have forfeited our natural access to all spiritual dimensions. By and by we have lost sight of these dimensions, until we eventually could not see, nor sense, nor perceive, nor experience them – at this crossroad we are presently standing as humanity.

Our organs to see, our organs of perception, though, are not taken from us, but we have lost the consciousness that it is not only natural to use them but that we moreover need them in order to be able to enter the wonder of being and to be carried anew again by life. In consequence these organs have regressed and as humanity we are only now engaged in discovering them anew.

This is the deep meaning of the current process of awakening.
It is high time we begin to sense again our insatiable desire for the connection with the divine, that we experience within the incarnated body the deep longing for our lost spiritual home on earth, then we shall wake again.

For this, though, we will have to free ourselves again from the fetters that we have voluntarily allowed to be put onto us by religious structures and institutions – in doing this we will again receive the direct access to the source. At this place begins the path to inner freedom.

We all have experiences with various religious institutions, even if in this life we are not connected to any of them. This fetter is imprinted like a code into our own system like an invisible seal. Through this we are all in the hands of such institutions, even if we don't at all want it any longer or believe we are inwardly free.
This demands from each one of us a very conscious step and above all a clear step.

This imprint resides within our heart, whether we believe this to be true or not. This place has clearly been chosen very well and consciously, because through this we are restricted, hindered and hampered in our most important strength, in our most important light. If our heart is not free, we cannot develop our presence to the fullest, no matter how much of an effort we make – we are not able to blossom.

I wish to give you a short description of how it is possible to shed this seal. As a support we can call on our personal companions and the non-incarnated souls. For this we connect ourselves very consciously with our personal angel presence and the personal elemental beings. We sense our deep roots that grow into the earth and the cosmos – we are anchored and present. Inwardly we imagine clearly what this is about and what we wish to achieve.

Then we sense how the light of our personal angel presence is condensing within our heart – so intensely that we are able to perceive it all the way into our physical sphere. Out of this a beam of light forms itself which encompasses our whole being and above all our heart-space. Through this we are sheltered and protected. We experience this light consciously.

When we are able to sense this condensing of the light well, we ask for this seal to become visible and noticeable for us within the strong light. Important here is that we create a conscious connection to our heart space. Thus we can locate the place accurately. With our inner eye we behold what kind of an energetic shape this code has. We take the code into our hands and allow it to dissolve through the powers, through the light, through the love, which flow from our heart and through our hands. We do this with a profound knowledge and consciousness that we have served these structures through many lifetimes and that now we wish to be independent and free in our being, in our own presence and in our spiritual consciousness. We should sense this event very precisely and decidedly in our body as well as showing it outwardly.

Then we can sense how the light within the most inner part of the spiritual ray in which we stand condenses even further and how the pure divine light touches our heart, our hands and the last remnants of the seal – like a drop of the purest dew, which purifies and cleanses everything to the end.

We ask for a clear sign so that we sense how we can rebuild the direct connection to the divine – now with a pure and out of a full heart.

In deep gratitude for this inner liberation we thank all the assisting beings for their support.

Thank you, Ajra, I sense, that this is very important. How would it feel if all humans were prepared to do this? That would be a collective liberation – and this is precisely what we are so longingly waiting for. How is it on the collective level – do we likewise have such an imprint, which constricts us and never allows us to breathe deeply? And can we change something about this as individual human beings?

It is unfortunately the case that we are collectively very strongly shaped by these religious structures. It is like an energetic grid, which has been put over us and keeps us confined within a frame that is too small for us.

As a picture we can imagine a very dense fog, which hangs over us and separates us from the spiritual dimensions – like a sort of damper, which ensures that we will not develop spiritually too far or too high. We are thereby being kept collectively in check.

In the same way that we have seals on the personal level, there are also similar collective seals, which constantly anchor and renew these structures. Through the large religious centres, as for example in Rome for the Catholic Church, they are anchored in the earth and hence also in the material world. Here they are like active acupuncture pressure points, which unfold a constant effect.

Another level is the set prayers, daily rituals and constant repetition of certain words. These create a carpet of fog, which constantly disturbs, guides into a certain direction or even just colours our spiritual connection to the divine, whether we want, notice or support this or not.

At present I observe mankind from a certain distance. Because I am not directly part of it I can tell you and must warn you that this fog has a much more potent impact than you are aware of! Take this seriously, as it concerns, directs and even manipulates your life immensely. And independently of how each one of us stands in this present life as regards church and religious institutions, we are all as it were collectively under this cover or lid.

Each person has her/his own path and therewith their own relationship, their own connection to the divine – for us humans as spiritual beings, it is impossible to not have a connection to the divine. There are of course big differences of how intense, how pure, how alive and how strong this connection is in this life.

But ALL human beings have the right to touch the divine in their own way and manner, to carry it within and bring it into life through their own being. There is no institution, no power in the world, which would have the authority to determine such for us. And it is in no way meant that we are being determined and manipulated by their rules.

We are spiritually independent beings and have no need of an intermediary and even less of someone who leads us into a certain direction.

I can tell you that through this fog life loses its shine and radiant colour, and I must admit this does say a lot about this fog. It is truly time to wake up!

Every human being who liberates her/himself personally, who manages to inwardly free her/himself, who finds her/his own luminous path as a connection to the divine, penetrates this fog and hence breaks through this cover. In this way ever more beams of light appear which cannot be darkened any more.
However, it is crucial to also work on energetically disabling the 'anchoring points' of these powers.

This does not mean that we wish to take the energy away from the institutions, instead we wish to claim our right to be spiritually free.

This is not something that, once attained, will remain forever, rather it needs to be constantly reinforced and renewed. We are dealing here with old structures, which have emerged throughout the long human history – these are relics of the past, from which we have to free ourselves now.

The religions, the churches are welcome to continue existing and operating; this does not interfere with anyone, as long as everyone is free to decide whether s/he wishes to belong to them or not.

I believe much will change, also on the collective level, once everyone recognises this seal on the personal level, transforms it and frees her/himself from it.

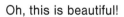

These are truly challenging themes...all this burdens us, even more so as we do not know much about them. We will surely return to the discussed themes because it is so valuable to view all of this from other perspectives.

But now changing the subject entirely, I would like to hear something beautiful about us human beings. Looking at us here on earth in our incarnated bodies, what do you see and experience as our greatest strength and most beautiful quality? What moves you the most? When do you sense us humans the strongest?

Oh, this is beautiful!

I am always moved when something truthful happens – the truth has a tremendous aura. She is like nourishment, which satisfies because it contains depth.

Feelings can be strong, but only move us when they are truthful.

I can tell you how it is for me. When the feelings are superficial or false, it is like being at a theatre performance with important dialogues but not hearing any sound. I do indeed notice that there are feelings, but they cannot move me. They are unreachable for me. Though they are at that moment real and present, they have no weight and do not leave a real trace behind within me – they dissolve without having moved anything.

Obviously the greatest strength we humans can develop is the power of the heart – and thus love! There is nothing more beautiful than to sense pure heart-love. This is the driving force and also the power that moves all of us the most. It is true bliss when I can experience the purity of love – in the etheric sphere the most beautiful coloured patterns, like mandalas, unfold out of her waves, which shine incredibly far.

The space which emerges from this is a pure channel, which opens and offers itself to the spirit world so that the spirit world may work through it.
It is very noticeable when a human being experiences this, and it is unspeakably beautiful and strong when several people experience this in a group. The impact, the waves, the light are unbelievable. We eminently underestimate the power of the heart.

The love of the heart is truly the power to open all doors – even if this is not always visible on the physical level. I can assure you that no deed, no work, no intention, no action that originates and happens from out of true heart's power will remain without an effect – the impulse of the heart is too powerful that its impact could stay invisible.

The true moments of love, which we can witness, are like what the shooting stars in the starry sky are for you. They are pure joy, and they are nourishment for us.

I can say to you that my only wish to return once more into my life would be to be able to tell this once more to the people I love but now with the knowledge I hold as a soul here in the spirit-all.

As incarnated human beings we are too little aware of how strong the power of love is and what effect she has. We believe it is self-evident that the others know we love them and hence we do not tell them. This, however, is sad, because in this way we do not allow the power of love to blossom.

When we love someone it is like a bud. The most beautiful bud, however, only opens properly, when we actively live this love – when we show it, when we express our feelings, when we radiate them.

Naturally an intense tranquil love is precious and strong, but it gains still another dimension when it shows herself and expands into the whole of the space around.

It is not a matter of telling everyone how much we love them, but even more about the living feeling of love, which we can express with our being even without words. It is about letting the impulse of love flow freely to enable it to form its own space.

We humans have forgotten how much more beautiful, fluid and simpler life would be, if we were to make use of our main organ, our heart, more actively. There is really no door that cannot be opened by the impulse of the heart.

This is our magic wand. As humans we can all perform magic, but we have forgotten that we have the wand and with it could do magic.

Are you able to give us more examples, images and concrete ideas as to how we can again learn to perform magic through love? How does the power of love work? How does the power of love flow and how is its effect in the invisible dimensions? We can't really see its true influence here on earth with our physical eyes. We all know that love is something noble, beautiful and strong, but we are nevertheless not yet conscious of what it is capable of moving.

Yes, it is well possible that you view love too narrowly.

Love is indeed an emotion that we can feel towards someone or something, but at the same time it is also the spark for the divine. This means that when we experience love we also unite ourselves directly with the creative power.

Of course this only holds true under the condition that the love is truthful. The feeling of love is often seen too personally, too tight, too much directed towards one person or condition. We do not need to be in love to feel a strong love.

In this sense love is meant more as a power than a feeling. Love is an

Entering into the love of the all-beingness

expression of our inner vitality and creativity – if we love life, if we love to live, then we can use this love as a magic power. Love then becomes the key that will help us everywhere and always.

For example, it is possible through a wave of love to support and carry into the world a project important to us. In this manner it will be entirely differently supported by the spiritual world and can bring more abundant fruits.
We can, for example, treat plants in our vegetable garden with the power of love – for this we do not need to be in love with them – and they will absorb the nutrients differently and be able to grow better.

When we view the power of love as a spark for the divine, we can understand this power differently. We carry the divine within us, we are the divine and can touch the divine within and around us best through pure love.

Why do we experience the world all pink when we are in love? Life then appears to be flowing and we experience that everything is much easier. This is not only because we are blinded and carried by the feeling of love, but because at this moment we move as it were in a cloud of love and hence are more open for the divine. Inwardly we are closer to the divine – we can sense it more intensely, no matter whether this happens consciously or unconsciously.

As souls we are at home in the divine; this is why we blossom as souls when we are closer to the divine. We are then quite differently nourished and can perceive, understand, live and love life on the earth so differently.
It is precisely for this reason love is the driving force and not because it makes us happy. Yes, it does indeed make us happy, but the reason is not the mere feeling of love, but because the power of love opens us for the divine impulse.

Everything we do in life we can do with or without the power of love, and it is just this that makes the biggest difference. Namely we open the divine gate, or we just don't. We open the space so that something significant, beautiful, pure, radiant can happen or we don't do this.
It is about the inner attitude, which we can freely choose as human beings,

or also not choose.

We can decide whether we take life as a dance of love and therewith fashion life in harmony with the divine or whether we see ourselves as victims of life who do not have much influence on the progress of our lives. This remains our free decision.

If it is indeed as you say that this is our free decision, one can hardly understand why not everyone chooses for love. Life on earth would indeed be so much more beautiful, fulfilling and simpler. How should I understand this? Are we so blind or so un-free, that we cannot decide freely after all?

I am so sorry, but we are again diverging from all that is beautiful about us humans...

Correct, it is in our hands, but we do not grasp it and continue to search for our happiness in the distance, instead of seeing that it is so very near.
As you already said, it is solely to do with our inner freedom. Ever and again it's about the same question: how much burden, how much in unresolved matters and how much ballast are we souls still hauling along with us?

True love we can only see and recognise if we also carry it within us. If our inner space is overcrowded with wounds, with old patterns, with memories of old misunderstandings in love relationships, then there is unfortunately no room for the power of love.

Love is such a subtle force; it can only exist when we are cleansed inwardly. Love demands from us much inner preparatory work, transformation and catharsis. She is like the crowning of life.

As non-incarnated souls we are embedded within the divine and hence love fills out most of our being. This is also our point of departure for the path of incarnation. At the moment of conception we are being connected to the concrete material world as souls and consequently more strongly influenced from this moment onwards by the physical events around us.

The big question is, how much of this love-substance, which filled us almost completely before our incarnation, are we able to retain until birth and then carry into life.

Several factors play into this. One of them is how far the soul is in her development – how far she has milled her experiences out of former lives and the phases in between. The more the soul has been incarnated and the more challenging the situations have been which she has mastered, the finer is her substance and the more direct her connection to the spiritual and the divine – through this the soul can anchor her love deeper into her own being and carry it into the incarnated life.

The second factor is the environment in which the soul lives through her incarnation process. The space could be open and prepared for the soul or the converse could be the case. A harmonious atmosphere filled with love might be prepared for the arriving soul, which would nourish and protect the love in this soul further, or the soul is confronted on her path with the opposite – which weakens and attacks her love.

A crucial factor is the birth process itself, as it can be a more fluid transition or a caesura, which strengthens or weakens her accordingly.

And it makes a great difference with how much love we begin our life within our fundamental substance. This is the foundation for our being, for our presence.

The more plentiful our reservoir of love, the more direct our spiritual connection will remain and therewith the more we will feel carried, present and nourished in life. In the other scenario we live with the feeling that we have to build up our reserves, and indeed with everything – with all that we give and with that which we receive from life or take for ourselves. We fail to notice how inexhaustible the fountain is .

Love grows the more we experience it and the more we let it flow on, bring it into motion, receive it – the more it can circulate. But it can only circulate in this way when, without a feeling of lack, we experience and live it in a constant flow.

Hence the substance of love that we are able to preserve throughout the process of incarnation of our soul is decisive for our whole life because it is the true foundation of life.

I find this does explain much in life. Something like this we humans here on earth are not conscious of anymore. By now we do know how important pregnancy is for the child, but mostly regarding the aspect, that in this way we prepare the path for the soul, that we hold the space, but I believe we are not conscious of how crucial a full reservoir of love is for the further course of life of this incarnating human being.

Could you further illuminate for us this connection between love and the divine? I find this so central as we see love too personally and limited to a small circle and hence forget that through it we are connected to the creation.

As a soul I am now embedded within the pure power of creation. This affords me the possibility to work through and digest the experiences, the emotions and happenings – all the soul-material that I have gathered throughout my life. If I may draw an amusing parallel: we humans are ruminators, like the cows, because we likewise chew continuously – except that we do not chew grass but ruminate on all that we have experienced.

I am now as soul very close to the divine because I am wholly spiritual substance. The more I process, the finer I am inwardly and hence the substance of love fills me the more and I am nearer to the divine.

The divine itself does not have any physical substance, so it can live wherever such fine weaving of love is formed. Thus it is very simple – the more love, the more divine presence.

The one or other might now ask: but why love in particular? Couldn't it just as well be the power of joy or the feeling of fulfilment or of happiness?

The true power of love is the purest power that exists. It is connected with the strength of the heart; we could say that it is being filtered and thereby even more purified by the heart.

When we look at joy or the feeling of happiness or any other feeling, which fills us humans and lifts us within our being, we also find within these the feeling of love. All of them contain the spark of love and so they all radiate through us because they fill our inner being.

Through love we arrive at our divine source and therewith at our origin. This is why we feel so at home when we are being loved.

When both the outer and the inner space are filled with the power of love, we are also again near to the soul condition in which I now dwell, and this brings us closer to ourselves as souls. It isn't just a memory, which arises within us, but a state in which we are completely free, held and protected and quite embedded in the divine as soul. One calls this the divine feeling of being-one.

It would take ever so little for us to experience this feeling of being supported much more often if not always. It is really very difficult to understand why humanity has lost this natural innate knowledge and that we are not conscious anymore that love can bring us so deep and far. We, humanity, have plain forgotten the simplest means, which can always help us.

We have lost the access to our own being. How do you see our path into the power of love? We all know we cannot go back, but how to continue?

The moment of shock will inevitably arrive – within and without – and through this the leaden layer, which makes us human beings so dulled and inwardly blind, will fall off. Then human beings will be searching again for the knowledge of the invisible. Life will be running its course again in its natural pathways and access to the different dimensions will become more accessible again.

As humanity we are definitely as yet not mature enough on the collective

The divine light

level. Only once the circumstances of our lives grow even tighter will we sense how un-free we have become within our being. To know that we are un-free does not seem to help us; evidently we need to truly experience and suffer this bondage so we can grasp it the more profoundly.

Viewed from without I can safely say: it cannot go on like this – our steps as humanity are currently clearly going backwards instead of forwards. Naturally these are unavoidable processes of maturation for our development, but in the overall process we will not advance in this way. Hence we can only hope that we will mature by way of these current challenges and so be able to advance further.

If the tendency towards self-destruction outweighs the possibility for development, there arises the necessity of a caesura, otherwise life is in danger.

And as humanity we are standing at such a turning point. Here we are coming back to the image of the jump across the abyss.
As humanity we have to renew and transform ourselves, because we are losing ourselves ever more. With this I do not only mean the everyday dimmed state, which I currently observe with the incarnated people, but above all I am thinking of the heartrending loss that we witness due to the many unnatural deaths and the partially fatal handling of death and its process, which is so important for the soul.

As long as the souls have the opportunity after the process of dying to go on their path into the peace of the all-being, they can compose themselves again and at least to a certain degree renew themselves and fill themselves with the impulse of love. Therewith the circle and flow of life is preserved, even if at times it has already been partially assailed. If this is, however, also no longer possible for the souls, it becomes critical and hence high time for a decisive change.

When the soul does not come to rest any longer to digest and integrate what she experienced in her deepest being, if instead of renewing herself she is dealing with composing and finding herself, if she is being interrupted continuously in her process, she will not return to her source, back to the creation-power, but will then be confused already at the very start of her new incarnation, is lost and no longer strongly enough connected with her source. For the soul this means an increasingly superficial experiencing of life.

And what we see at present everywhere in the world is an inevitable result of this. However much we would wish to, we could no longer enter deeply enough into life, because as souls we have already neither the peace nor the strength and as human beings can't anymore develop much further the capability to love. Life plays out ever more merely on the surface and the power of love becomes ever shallower and weaker, in consequence of which we collectively and increasingly lose our knowledge of belonging to the divine.

This is not only critical but tragic. Hence the logical consequence is that a decisive change of our being as humans is absolutely indispensable.

Are we able to prepare ourselves for this? How could we be one step ahead? What is important – what brings us nearer to what is currently happening? What is most essential at this moment, and what should our inner gaze orientate itself towards right now? Is there something that could help us?

Outwardly life continues, but inwardly a new space should develop. A space which should grow ever wider and brighter, which will show itself initially as an empty space. The most important thing here is indeed that it remains entirely free – uncoloured, unadorned, unencumbered and truly pure.

Your task is to find the point out of which this space can develop and then to protect the developing purity. This is about a very conscious experiencing and inner presence – the more consciously we experience and carry this, the more clearly we will be able to take the further steps.

We currently need this space as protection for our inner core, but also in a certain way as a basis, which will serve later on as the foundation for the arising of the new.

This is no passive empty space, but rather within it lives a highly active pull of life energy, that in spite of its enormous breadth and openness creates a potentised intensity. We really should protect this space consciously and actively, as it plays a unique role in our further development.

We will sense and know precisely, when the moment has come that we can offer this space as fruitful earth, out of which something new can grow.

We believe that the connection to the spiritual world or likewise to the divine serves primarily so that we receive important information or guidance, and yet we forget that above all we get closer to our own wellspring and to ourselves through this connection – we ourselves become more a part of the spiritual sphere.
The spiritual spheres are our home. We renew, nourish and strengthen our souls every time we enter into the calm of the spiritual space.

Here we should not forget that as humanity we are anchoring ourselves ever deeper into physical matter and therefore need an ever more direct access to the spiritual dimensions. Just now, however, the opposite occurs – if we compare how strongly we as civilisation were previously connected to the spiritual spheres, how we were likewise connected with the sphere of the non-incarnated souls, we unfortunately observe that the connection is getting weaker rather than stronger.

The main question in human life is: how far am I connected with my true being – for the more connected I am the more awake and strongly I can play my role in life and for life.
To come closer to my soul being I need the soul to be near to my source.

And here we arrive again at the point, how important the sphere of the non-incarnated souls is at present for the currently incarnated human beings: we are nearest to you in the spiritual spheres and hence also most easily reachable. We can be the doorway into eternity for you. We are the bridge that offers you the possibility to expand further into the spiritual dimensions. When this bridge is missing, as we experience right now, then the spiritual world is so much more difficult to reach for you. And this demands an

As support for current times

unequally stronger, more conscious striving for you humans to arrive at a similar spiritual openness to what you would have under normal circumstances.

That there are simultaneously incarnated and non-incarnated souls is a divine work, it could not be better. We are a perfect orchestra that assembles and covers all voices, we should just come together and recognise each other again.

I do not say this because I miss you humans, but because I can experience so clearly from my perspective how complete the tableau is when all souls – incarnated and currently non-incarnated – stand and work together. It results in such perfect harmony of which only such a highly gifted orchestra, as we humans are, is capable.

And the most unbelievable fact is that it would need so little to break again through the barrier that separates us – just one step. To express this with an image, we could say that we are now two separate light-spheres: one so to speak is sticking to the earth and the other stands alone in the all-beingness. Thereby each side is robbed of the elements represented by the other, instead of us continually mutually fertilising each other and enabling one another to expand further and to bring the meaning of life to blossom even more beautifully.

I hope very much that with all these thoughts, images and words I manage to make clearer to you why we belong together, why we need one another and how much potential we can activate together.

Life is so beautiful, but it could be even more beautiful, and the question addressed to everyone individually is: what does hinder me to take this step? What am I prepared to change for this?
To emphasise once more, so little is lacking here - just a conscious step!

That is not too much to ask, is it?

This reunification is going to be one of the great revolutions for mankind. It will allow us to answer the question about the abyss, which we have puzzled on at the beginning of this conversation, and assist us to effortlessly overcome this abyss. We are capable of so much more as humanity than we can believe or imagine.

You currently incarnated humans lack the boundless spiritual component to be able to leap and finally fly, and we can offer this.

Our hand is stretched out towards you, we are ready and are waiting for you, dear human beings.

This does give hope and confidence that humanity will manage. In the name of the incarnated portion I now say YES to this mutual path, in the hope that we will be an ever greater number who will recognise the necessity for this step.
We have addressed and touched upon many themes; what I am still interested in is how you perceive this most beautiful planet from your perspective. How do you perceive its development and in what way are we being challenged because of it?

One counts the earth as just one among many planets, but this is wrong. The earth isn't just one of the planets; the earth is the planet!

We aren't at all conscious of what the real function of the earth is. Do you think that it is coincidence that the earth has a magnetic field all around it or that there is exactly enough oxygen, or that there is water in unbelievable amounts, or that the sunlight is so critically tuned? There are too many coincidences for them to be simply coincidences.

The earth is in a spiritual sense the great sage in the collective of planets – she is a reflection of the whole universe and the spiritual embodiment of the All-beingness. These aren't just big words, this is the reality. The earth is the collection of all the qualities of life. It is also no coincidence that we speak of paradise in connection with the earth because it truly possesses the potential for this.

The earth and the life it enables through its being is a unique miracle. No matter which way you turn, if you look with an open mind you will recognise everywhere true miracles. It would be so wonderful, if only you would become conscious of what privilege you have to be living on this highly developed planet.

But what I tell you is nothing new – hence I wish to present the earth to you from my viewpoint. As with us humans, so also the earth is pure condensed light. To be sure, the sun endows the earth with light, but it only looks like this on the physical plane; on the spiritual level the earth radiates much stronger than the sun itself. The earth's etheric presence and therewith its energetic sphere is so luminous, you cannot possibly imagine it.

The most fascinating thing is that its spiritual presence is embodied in matter. It is the pure light, which was able to materialise more and more tangibly over millennia – until it had condensed so far that it became physical matter. earth that you can hold in your hands is pure light, which is why she is so fertile: it is actually gold.
When I observe the earth I see a radiant crystal, in which light is condensed, materialises itself, in which light is reflected and which continuously radiates light.

You think the earth exists so that it can serve us humans as a foundation for life, as basis for our nourishment, but the true picture is somewhat different. Actually we humans can be grateful that we are able to serve this miracle with our being.

Another image for this: the whole universe is reflected and imprints itself into the earth, it mirrors itself in every single cell of the earth – hence we can say: in our cells the entire universe mirrors itself by way of the earth.

From this perspective we are suddenly no longer victims of life, beings who landed on earth by chance and now need to fight for our survival. No, we are nothing less than an image of the universe and are being constantly shone through as if through a spiritual prism, due to the presence of the earth. Because of this we are not only part of the universe, but rather mirror ourselves within this play of light simultaneously in the earth and in the cosmos – thereby we influence life by way of our individual footsteps.

I believe we are far too little conscious of how strong this connection between us human beings and the earth is. This is a further spiritual separation, which limits us a lot – time and again we go against the flow and thereby weaken this working together.

The earth is a miracle and we human beings are also a miracle – together we can forge a most beautiful life. We ONLY lack the consciousness for this.

Could you give us some more examples and images with regards to this, please. We are becoming ever more conscious of the fact that the earth is not only a living organism but a being. However, this being is so vast that it by far surpasses our imagination. Could you maybe bring this being a bit closer to us, so that we may grasp and understand better what this in fact means for us humans?

The earth is not only lived upon by many beings but is itself a living being. How can we imagine this?

When I view the earth as a whole I can see that life is coordinated, the course of life is cared for, life revolves in cycles, which are not left to chance – there is a clear and healthy structure, which supports and guides life on earth.
This indicates that there is a higher intelligence behind what we see. Of course all that I have mentioned here is being attributed to the biological nature of the planet. Well, that is true, but without a higher being of intelligence, which coordinates all integrated levels with one another, life on earth would have long since collapsed.

Life on earth does not revolve in circles but in a continuously ascending spiral and this also can only occur because there is a higher entity, which guides this on-going growth and evolution and therewith enables the growth of all of us, as part of this organism.

I obviously could paint you a most beautiful, nearly kitschy picture of this being, but I rather describe it as pure divine light, which I perceive in the core of the earth. It is the most beautiful light I have ever seen.

The earth has such a pure and sacred core, that she cannot possibly be destroyed. One is talking so much about the destruction of this planet, but I can say with full confidence that there is no serious danger, because the earth is so strong. There would be a problem only if for some reason one were able to pollute the innermost core of the earth.

The earth is the planet of learning, therefore she must have the capacity to deal with certain failed attempts and failures. The earth's power to heal and her creativity are greater than the devastation we humans cause.
This does not mean, however, that we humans can disrespectfully, callously and with egoistic self-interest completely destroy everything ! I only wish to say that the earth has a lot of patience with us humans, because we need this exercise field – we not only learn in our own personal setting but also as civilisation.

The main injuries occur mainly because we are not in a position to see the earth as one large whole. We always view merely our own home, one landscape, one country, one continent, but completely forget that all of it and more belong to a greater whole.

We can compare it with our body: we also sense if someone pulls on our left ear or tickles our large toe – everything that happens throughout and around the whole of our body, we sense, because all our parts are connected. Likewise a happening on one side of the earth influences the happenings on the other side – it is one organism, one unit, one happening.

I have described that we humans are light and come out of the divine all-beingness when we are incarnating on earth. We manifest ourselves as light on earth, but for this we also need the miracle light of the earth.
I have also said that the earth is condensed and materialised light and to achieve this she has gone through a lengthy development. She has thereby undergone the alchemy of turning the gold-light into her own substance,

which we experience again at every birth and every death – this emerging and dematerialising are possible solely through the being and wisdom of the earth. How could for example a physical body materialise at the moment of conception other than through an alchemical process, which is only possible by the power and magic of the earth?

We can come up with many theories of how life arises and explain it ever so scientifically, but if we look more closely, we will notice that we do not really have a true explanation for how a soul finds herself suddenly again within a physical body in the process of incarnating. This is a synthesis of the highest order, which we cannot characterise with any physical, biological or any scientific concepts. It is a miracle that can only happen in the lap of the earth because she is initiated as a being into the deepest alchemical knowledge – she herself is the expression of this wisdom.

We are so naïve to think that we reproduce ourselves out of our own drive, that we develop out of our own impulse, that we merely out of our own wish incarnate here on earth or that we are capable of walking through our own knowledge and forget hereby that we can do all this and much more only because we are embedded into this immense being – the earth.
A path of incarnation is not just a miracle work of humanity but one of humanity within the field of consciousness of the earth. A birth is not just a biological event, but is a miracle, which is only possible in this fashion on planet earth. Do you understand what I mean by this?

Many incidents we ascribe to the skills of human beings alone; in reality, however, they are only possible in the force field of the earth. This by no means puts our own merits into question, but far too often we forget the participation of the powers of the earth, which add their magic, so that which we could never accomplish on our own can happen.

The earth is not only the vessel, as we often hear in spiritual circles, she also adds much to its content. If we look once more at the miracle of the human incarnation process, we can say that half of it we bring as souls, the other half the earth adds with her presence.

Our miracle planet earth

With our existence as humans we are truly earth as much as we are also cosmos, and yet the earth is of course a separate being that exists beyond our being. But as we are as humanity part of this planetary system, we are in the care of its being.

As human beings we are of course free beings, follow our own path of development, have free power of decision, are creative, build and fashion out of our own impulses, and YET as part of this planet we are embedded within the impulses of the earth and therewith in her striving for growth and wish for development – this means that we are thriving underneath the vast 'protective shield' of the earth and without knowing it we are doing much out of this deep drive of the earth.

If we observe the big current wave of change: there is of course our human wish to grow, to develop ourselves further, to change the world situation, but let us not forget that there is just as much a motion of change coming out of the earth, which strongly affects our inner and outer movements. The earth is currently giving the impulse for this great leap – which does not only concern us as civilisation but all of us as dwellers on this planet.

The earth has been preparing the circumstances, scope and possible solutions for this universal change for some time. Precisely for this reason the current process of change is inevitable – though we can take some detours and slow down the process; if we absolutely wish to do so we can resist. But we cannot escape this process, because it has been set in motion by a higher entity, on which we have no influence.

So it helps if we tune ourselves in to find the inner access to this happening and join in. The more we are in the centre of this happening, the stronger we will be taken along and supported.

 Yes, we are truly great masters in overlooking the larger context – we believe that just we personally and as humanity undergo this great change, whilst actually we are embedded within something much bigger. If we manage to hold this great image

and to follow it, it will become much easier, because then we know that we are not alone, that much greater powers, which are moving in the same direction as us, are part of the event. What could you give us as inner aid, as tools? Do you have concrete images, ideas, thoughts, indications that can give us support and assistance in the current events?

Do not merely glance at your own feet, where you direct your steps, look forward, then you will be able to see the direction as a streaming of light. It is prepared, it is paved and hence clearly recognisable and visible, obviously for those who are prepared to glance a bit further.

The change happening right now is not against but for life, therefore there is ample support from all directions and dimensions – keep your eyes open and you will be able to discover signs everywhere. We are not alone in this event.

We are condensed light and originate from divine love. This means we are being carried in our core as long as we hold the connection to our source. We are protected and carried within the depth of our being.

When we remain in this feeling, no outer shocks, disturbances, projections, fears and falsehoods can disturb us. We will be able to freely follow the inner impulse. What else do we need? Do we need more than that?

This is the highest surety that will ever be given to us.

The only thing really demanded of us is that we decide what we stand for in life. When we sense love as our innermost nature, we know what is important to us and why we are here. When we are conscious of the light that we are, we know that at every moment we are carrying the light into life through our being. It is not a question of what we do but how we do it.

When we follow the light within us we serve the divine love. Then life will afford us ample opportunities and prepare us, so that we may anchor our inner truth as soul even deeper within ourselves and embody ever more light on the earth.

As souls we ALL follow this direction – to anchor ever more light within us, to carry it into matter, to cause it to radiate. As souls we have this orientation. How we conduct our life depends on the individual decisions we take in daily life.

Do not wait for an impetus from without; we are in the midst of this happening. We are called to be present, awake and active and indeed everywhere and with everything we do! Attempt to live ever more with this consciousness and you will be carried and guided always and everywhere.
This is the truly new consciousness – to be in high presence and openness: and indeed in the here and now!

Make use of life to gather new experiences as soul – not only as human being, and you will see how much life will change for you through this. There are so many possibilities for how to observe, an endless breadth of perspectives to view life from.

Life is indeed a serious endeavour, absolutely true, but do not take it too seriously – in the sense that life should always be taken as an experiment; one should feel free enough to experiment and to deal playfully with what life has to offer.

Ajra, I thank you! I have the feeling that this is well rounded off for now. We can continue anytime, if we see that people like reading these conversations.
You have opened new doors for us in many respects, you have given us some thoughts to 'keep on thinking' about, you have opened a new inner breadth and gifted us with a new image of humanity.
I am deeply grateful to you and believe I can equally say this in the name of many readers.

Thank you!!

I am also happy and grateful because I have the opportunity to be heard again. This is the reason why I am in the position that I am in right now as soul, hence I say thank you to you, too, Ana and to all who will read these words, thoughts and ideas, and will realise them in life and carry them further into life. THANK YOU.

I am looking forward to all the beauty that awaits us in the near future as humanity.

Ajra's presence

On the drawings:

When I was sixteen years old, I discovered the possibility of communicating with the other worlds. Already then I was introduced into the language of drawings. The energetic messages from out of other worlds, dimensions or other beings are never fixed within words but exist in energy-forms. Only when we take them into our material dimension do they acquire a concrete solid shape. Hence it is possible to translate one and the same spiritual or energetic message into many varying forms and languages. Words, drawings, music, cosmograms or paintings are such differing forms of expression, and yet they can all be carriers of the same stream of energy.

The drawings are a help for connecting, for example, more closely with the soul of Ajra, with the different themes discussed in the text, and for entering then into a more intimate exchange with these. We can use them like inner keys, which will help us to reach ever further and deeper.

It is not like drawing automatically, because I have kept a conscious connection with Ajra's soul, with a specific theme and beings, which were helping, so that I was actively involved in the process of this emergence. My hand is being physically guided in the process. The beginning of the drawing is always being connected to the end of the line.

The two small drawings (one for Ajra and one for me) are also developed in the same way.

Here I give a suggestion to how one could use the drawings. The most important thing is to open oneself to force which radiates through the drawings and to allow yourself to be touched deeply within your heart. To deepen this connection ever further you can imagine a radiating sun within your heart, out of which you direct one ray onto a point in your chosen drawing. With this beam of light and your gaze you follow the line in the drawing for a while in your own rhythm, until you sense that your heart has opened and the connection between the heart and the drawing is created. All that you still need to do now is let the power stream. Another possibility is to photocopy the drawings and to colour them in following your own intuition. One can imagine these drawings as a gateway, through which we can gaze into the other dimensions. At the same time the other worlds obtain through this an opportunity to make contact with our world.

Ana Pogačnik

About the authors

Ana Pogačnik

1973 born in Slovenia

Seminar leader, author, mother of two small girls.

First I dedicated my life to the piano, later I studied archaeology.

Since 1989 I have been receiving messages from various spiritual sources.

Since 1999 I give seminars on the received knowledge about the invisible dimensions of the landscape and the mirroring thereof in us as human beings. While I lived abroad I founded Schule Wieder Sehen ('School to see Again') as a frame for this, which I then re-named to 'Modra Zemlja' (translated: Wise/Blue Earth), because I now live with my family in Slovenia.

Books: "How wide the heart", 2006* (only book published in English – written together with my father); in German I have published two more books in the last years.

More information at: www.ana-pogacnik.com

* *How Wide the Heart: The Roots of Peace in Palestine and Israel*, by Marko Pogačnik and Ana Pogačnik, Lindisfarne Books, 2006

Ajra Pogačnik

1967 born in Slovenia
2011 died

Healer, seminar leader, author, mother of two now grown up children.

As an exceptional healer she helped incredibly many people in her praxis.

She received diverse messages from out of the spiritual world and published two books about these.

She wrote two book, but they were not translated into English.

Acknowledgements

First of all I wish to give thanks from the bottom of my heart to my family, *Thomas, Klara* and *Eva*. Without your support I could not have fulfilled this and many other tasks. You are my most important life-pillars, which give colour and light to life. THANK YOU TO YOU, that we tread this path together!

Deep gratitude goes to my parents, *Marika* and *Marko*. It is of great help to know, that I am being supported by you in all that I do. Thank you that you have given us so much freedom as children, so that we could find ourselves.

I would like to give a huge thank to *Richard Brinton* to decide to publish the book in English and for the editing. You've done such a great work! And a thank you to *Zita Weckenmann* who also assisted in the process.

A great and heartfelt thanks goes to many *friends,* who support my and our work. It is indescribably beautiful to sense that we are many who walk this path −each on their own and yet united. I can no longer imagine myself facing all the challenges of our time without all of you. THANK YOU!

Further titles by InterActions

For more information and a complete listing
see https://interactions360.org

CORONA AND THE HUMAN HEART:
Illuminating riddles of immunity, conscience and common sense

by Michaela Glöckler, MD
with a Foreword by Branko Furst, MD

2021. ISBN 978-0-9528364-5-2, Pb 96 pp,
with colour and B&W illustrations, UK £7.95

New inspiring research on the significant role of the heart in the development of the immune system and the importance this understanding has for health and for the Covid crisis. The author leads us on a path showing how by strengthening our inner spiritual self – our inner sun – we will be strengthening our health and immunity, as well as illuminating riddles of conscience and common sense.

"This timely book represents a breakthrough in phenomenological research that will provide far-reaching insights not only to those who are prompted by the Corona pandemic to ask deeper questions related to health and medical freedom, but also to all open-minded researchers in pursuit of bridging the mind-body divide."
Branko Furst, MD, author of The Heart and Circulation: An integrative model.

WHAT COVID-19 CAN TEACH US
Meeting the virus with fear or informed common sense?

by Thomas Hardtmuth, MD.
Foreword by Michaela Glöckler, MD.

2021. ISBN 978-0-9528364-4-5, Pb 96 pp, UK £7.50

Dr Hardtmuth provides a detailed, highly readable analysis of the multi-dimensional Corona crisis, including an in-depth view of our immune system resilience with the latest science recognising viruses not as 'enemies' but as vital for human evolution and health. This holistic perspective suggests new approaches not only for treatment but also prevention. He examines further details around the Covid pandemic including the PCR test reliability, risks and benefits of vaccination, and fear's negative effect on immunity.

EDUCATION FOR THE FUTURE:
How to nurture health and human potential

by Michaela Glöckler, MD

2020, 2022. ISBN 978-0-9528364-3-8, Pb 248 pp, with colour photos and illustrations, UK £19.99.

'Almost every day you can read somewhere that a fundamental change is needed in schools and the education system... With this book it is my deep wish to make a contribution to this.'
M. Glöckler

Education for the Future is a plea for radically aligning upbringing and education with what is needed for the healthy development and well-being of children and adolescents. A unique contribution of Dr Glöckler is a year-by-year examination of human biological development and how this relates to soul-spiritual development, which in turn has a direct bearing on the needs of the child within upbringing and education.

This is a treasure chest of information and insights, and highly recommended for anyone working with children, whether as parent, teacher, carer, therapist or researcher, exploring from a holistic perspective the deep-seated issues of education for nurturing health, well-being and human potential.

GROWING UP HEALTHY IN A WORLD OF DIGITAL MEDIA
A guide for parents and caregivers of children and adolescents

Written by specialists from 15 organisations concerned with childhood development.
Introduction by Dr Michaela Glöckler, Pediatrician

2019. ISBN 9780 9528364 14, Pb sewn 160 pp, UK £10 with colour illustrations and photos, UK £10.

With increased screen use from the epidemic lockdowns, this new guide is more relevant than ever. It explains essential child development considerations for an age appropriate use of digital media. The risks from inappropriate use of digital media are considerable. This book offers practical advice to parents and teachers, divided according to children's age groups. Easy to read. *An essential guide.*